W9-CLB-887

3RD EDITION

Linux Pocket Guide

Daniel J. Barrett

Beijing · Boston · Farnham · Sebastopol · Tokyo

Linux Pocket Guide

by Daniel J. Barrett

Printed in the United States of America.

Published by O'Reilly Media, Inc., 1005 Gravenstein Highway North, Sebastopol, CA 95472.

O'Reilly books may be purchased for educational, business, or sales promotional use. Online editions are also available for most titles (*http://safaribooksonline.com*). For more information, contact our corporate/institutional sales department: 800-998-9938 or *corporate@oreilly.com*.

Editor: Nan Barber
Production Editor: Nicholas Adams
Copyeditor: Jasmine Kwityn
Proofreader: Susan Moritz
Indexer: Daniel Barrett
Interior Designer: David Futato
Cover Designer: Karen Montgomery
Illustrator: Rebecca Demarest

June 2016:   Third Edition

Revision History for the Third Edition
          2016-05-27:   First Release

See   *http://oreilly.com/catalog/errata.csp?isbn=9781491927571*   for   release
details.

978-1-491-92757-1

[M]

Table of Contents

Linux Pocket Guide

Welcome to Linux! If you're a new user, this book can serve as a quick introduction, as well as a guide to common and practical commands. If you have Linux experience, feel free to skip the introductory material.

What's in This Book?

This book is a short guide, *not a comprehensive reference*. We cover important, useful aspects of Linux so you can work productively. We do not, however, present every single command and every last option (our apologies if your favorite was omitted), nor delve into detail about operating system internals. Short, sweet, and essential—that's our motto.

We focus on *commands*, those pesky little words you type on a command line to tell a Linux system what to do. Here's an example command that counts lines of text in a file, *myfile*:

```
wc -l myfile
```

We'll cover the most important Linux commands for the average user, such as ls (list files), grep (search for text), mplayer (play audio and video files), and df (measure free disk space). We touch only briefly on graphical windowing environments like GNOME and KDE, each of which could fill a *Pocket Guide* by itself.

We've organized the material by function to provide a concise learning path. For example, to help you view the contents of a file, we introduce many file-viewing commands together: cat for short text files, less for longer ones, od for binary files, and so on. Then we explain each command in turn, briefly presenting its common uses and options.

We assume you have access to a Linux system and know how to log in with your username and password. If not, get your hands on a Linux "live" DVD, such as Ubuntu (*http://ubuntu.com/download*), Fedora (*https://getfedora.org/*), or Knoppix (*http://www.knopper.net/knoppix/index-en.html*), which you can boot on most computers to play around with Linux.

What's New in the Third Edition?

New commands

Technology changes quickly, and some commands that made sense to cover in the first two editions are barely used today. We've replaced these commands with new ones that you'll find immediately practical on a modern Linux system.

Runnable examples

You can now download a set of files from the book's website (*http://linuxpocketguide.com/*) and run the book's example commands as you read them.

Goodbye, GUI applications

We no longer cover applications that have graphical user interfaces, such as photo editors and web browsers, in order to focus purely on commands. You can find these applications yourself pretty easily these days just by searching the Web.

What's Linux?

Linux is a popular, open source operating system that competes with Microsoft Windows and Mac OS X. Like these other operating systems, Linux has a graphical user interface with windows, icons, and mouse control. However, the real power of Linux comes from its command-line interface, called the *shell*, for typing and running commands like the preceding wc.

Windows and Mac OS X computers can be operated by command line as well (Windows with its cmd and PowerShell command tools, and OS X with its Terminal application), but most of their users can get along fine without typing commands. On Linux, the shell is critical. If you use Linux without the shell, you are missing out.

What's a Distro?

Linux is extremely configurable and includes thousands of programs. As a result, different varieties of Linux have arisen to serve different needs and tastes. They all share certain core components but may look different and include different programs and files. Each variety is called a *distro* (short for "distribution"). Popular distros include Ubuntu Linux, Red Hat Enterprise Linux, Slackware, and Mint among others. This book covers core material that should apply to every distro.

What's a Command?

A Linux command typically consists of a *program name* followed by *options* and *arguments*, typed within a shell, like this:

```
wc -l myfile
```

The program name (wc, short for "word count") refers to a program somewhere on disk that the shell will locate and run. Options, which usually begin with a dash, affect the behavior of the program. In the preceding command, the -l option tells wc to count lines and not words. The argument myfile specifies the file that wc should read and process.

Commands can have multiple options and arguments. Options may be given individually:

```
wc -l -w myfile                Two individual options
```

or combined after a single dash:

```
wc -lw myfile          Same as -l -w
```

though some programs are quirky and do not recognize combined options. Multiple arguments are also OK:

```
wc -l myfile myfile2          Count lines in two files
```

Options are not standardized. They may be a single dash and one character (say, -l), two dashes and a word (--lines), or several other formats. The same option may have different meanings to different programs: in the command wc -l, the option -l means "lines of text," but in ls -l it means "longer output." Two programs also might use different options to mean the same thing, such as -q for "run quietly" versus -s for "run silently." Some options are followed by a value, such as -s 10, and space between them might not be required (-s10).

Likewise, arguments are not standardized. They usually represent filenames for input or output, but they can be other things too, like directory names or regular expressions.

Commands can be more interesting than just a single program with options:

- Commands can run several programs at a time, either in sequence (one program after another) or in a "pipeline" with the output of one command becoming the input of the next. Linux experts use pipelines all the time.

- The Linux command-line user interface—the *shell*—has a programming language built in. So instead of a command saying "run this program," it might say, "run this program, write its output to a file of my choosing, and if any errors occur, send me an email with the results."

Shell prompts

Before you can type a command, you must wait for the shell to display a special symbol, called a *prompt*. A prompt means, "I am waiting for your next command." Prompts come in all shapes and sizes, depending on how your shell is configured. Your prompt might be a dollar sign:

```
$
```

or a complex string of text containing your computer name, username, and possibly other information and symbols:

```
myhost:~smith$
```

or various other styles. All these prompts mean the same thing: the shell is ready for your commands.

In this book, we'll use the unique symbol → to indicate a shell prompt, so you won't mistakenly type it as part of a command. Here is a prompt followed by a command:

```
→ wc -l myfile
```

Some commands will print text on the screen as they run. To distinguish your command (which you type) from its printed output (which you don't), we'll display the command in bold like this:

```
→ wc -l myfile          The command you type
18 myfile               The output it produces
```

Some commands in this book can be run successfully only by an *administrator*, a special user with permission to do anything on the system. (Such a user is also called a *superuser* or *root*.) In this case, we precede the command with sudo:

```
→ sudo superuser command goes here
```

We'll discuss sudo fully in "Becoming the Superuser" on page 170, but for now, all you need to know is that sudo gives you superpowers and sometimes will prompt for your password. For example, to count lines in a protected file called */etc/shadow*, with and without sudo, you could run this command:

```
→ wc -l /etc/shadow               This will fail
wc: /etc/shadow: Permission denied
→ sudo wc -l /etc/shadow          Now with sudo
```

```
Password: *******
51 /etc/shadow                    It worked!
```

Command-line warm-up

To give you a feel for Linux, here are 10 simple commands you can try right now. You must type them *exactly*, including capital and small letters, spaces, and all symbols after the prompt.

Display a calendar for April 2017:

```
→ cal apr 2017
     April 2017
Su Mo Tu We Th Fr Sa
                   1
 2  3  4  5  6  7  8
 9 10 11 12 13 14 15
16 17 18 19 20 21 22
23 24 25 26 27 28 29
30
```

List the contents of the */bin* directory, which contains many commands:

```
→ ls /bin
bash      less       rm
bunzip2   lessecho   rmdir
busybox   lessfile   rnano
...
```

Count the number of visible items in your home directory (represented here by a special variable HOME that we'll discuss later):

```
→ ls $HOME | wc -l
8
```

See how much space is used on a partition of your hard disk:

```
→ df -h /
Filesystem  Size  Used Avail Use% Mounted on
/dev/sdb1   78G   30G   48G  61% /
```

Watch the processes running on your computer (type "q" to quit):

```
→ top -d1
```

Print the file */etc/hosts*, which contains names and addresses of computers, on your default printer if you have one set up:

```
→ lpr /etc/hosts
```

See how long you've been logged in:

```
→ last -1 $USER
smith   pts/7 :0   Tue Nov 10 20:12   still logged in
```

Download a file *sample.pdf* from this book's website to your current directory, without needing a web browser:

```
→ wget http://linuxpocketguide.com/sample.pdf
```

Display information about your computer's IP address:

```
→ ip addr show eth0
...
inet 192.168.1.47
```

See who owns the domain name *oreilly.com* (press the space bar to move forward page by page, and type "q" to quit):

```
→ whois oreilly.com | less
Domain Name: OREILLY.COM
Registrar: GODADDY.COM, LLC
...
```

Finally, clear the window:

```
→ clear
```

OK, that was more than 10 commands...but congratulations: you are now a Linux shell user!

Reading This Book

We'll describe many Linux commands in this book. Each description begins with a standard heading about the command; Figure 1 shows one for the ls (list files) command. This heading demonstrates the general usage in a simple format:

```
ls [options] [files]
```

which means you'd type "ls" followed, if you choose, by options and then filenames. You wouldn't type the square brackets "[" and "]": they just indicate their contents are optional; and words in italics mean you have to fill in your own specific values, like names of actual files. If you see a vertical bar between options or arguments, perhaps grouped by parentheses:

```
(file | directory)
```

this indicates choice: you may supply either a filename or directory name as an argument.

Figure 1. Standard command heading

The special heading in Figure 1 also includes six properties of the command printed in black (supported) or gray (unsupported):

stdin

> The command reads from standard input (i.e., your keyboard), by default. See "Input and Output" on page 15.

stdout

> The command writes to standard output (i.e., your screen), by default. See "Input and Output" on page 15.

- file

> When given a dash (-) argument in place of an input filename, the command reads from standard input; and likewise, if the dash is supplied as an output filename, the command writes to standard output. For example, the fol-

lowing `wc` command line reads the files *myfile* and *myfile2*, then standard input, then *myfile3*:

```
wc myfile myfile2 - myfile3
```

-- opt

> If you supply the command-line option "--" it means "end of options": anything appearing later on the command line is not an option. This is sometimes necessary to work with a file whose name begins with a dash, which otherwise would be (mistakenly) treated as an option. For example, if you have a file named *-dashfile*, the command `wc -dashfile` will fail because `-dashfile` will be treated as an (invalid) option. `wc -- -dashfile` works. If a command does not support "--", you can prepend the current directory path "./" to the filename so the dash is no longer the first character:

```
wc ./-dashfile
```

`--help`

> The option `--help` makes the command print a help message explaining proper usage, then exit.

`--version`

> The option `--version` makes the command print its version information and exit.

Keystrokes

Throughout the book, we use certain symbols to indicate keystrokes. Like many other Linux documents, we use the ^ symbol to mean "press and hold the Control (Ctrl) key," so for example, ^D (pronounced "control D") means "press and hold the Control key and type D." We also write ESC to mean "press the Escape key." Keys like Enter and the space bar should be self-explanatory.

Your friend, the echo command

In many of our examples, we'll print information to the screen with the echo command, which we'll formally describe in "Screen Output" on page 203. echo is one of the simplest commands—it merely prints its arguments on standard output, once those arguments have been processed by the shell:

```
→ echo My dog has fleas
My dog has fleas
→ echo My name is $USER          Shell variable USER
My name is smith
```

Long command lines

Sometimes, a command will be too lengthy to fit on one line in the book. In these cases, we'll split the command onto multiple lines that end with a backward slash character:

```
→ echo This is a long command that doesn't fit on \
  one line
This is a long command that doesn't fit on one line
```

This is not merely a helpful notation: the backslash character actually serves this purpose in the Linux shell, as a "line continuation" character. Of course, if your terminal is wider than this page, you can omit the backslash and just type the whole command on one line.

Practicing with This Book

This book comes with a collection of files for practicing with Linux. If you download these files and install them on any Linux machine, then you can run most of the example com-

mands in this book verbatim. To download these files for the
first time, run these commands:[1]

```
→ cd
→ wget http://linuxpocketguide.com/LPG-stuff.tar.gz
→ tar -xf LPG-stuff.tar.gz
```

These commands create a directory named *linuxpocketguide* in
your home directory. Any time you see an example command
in this book, simply visit this new directory:

```
→ cd ~/linuxpocketguide
```

and run the example command.

As you practice, if you'd like to re-download and install the
examples (say, if you've modified some example files and want
a fresh start), simply run the reset-lpg script located in the
linuxpocketguide directory:

```
→ cd ~/linuxpocketguide
→ bash reset-lpg
```

If you have placed the examples somewhere other than your
home directory (implying that you are already comfortable
with Linux directories), supply that directory name as an argument to the reset-lpg command:

```
→ bash reset-lpg /tmp/examples
```

This command would create or refresh the examples in the
directory */tmp/examples/linuxpocketguide*.

Getting Help

If you need more information than this book provides, there
are several things you can do.

---

1 Alternatively, you can download the example files from *https://
github.com/oreillymedia/linux_pocket_guide*.

Run the man *command*

The man command displays an online manual page, or *manpage*, for a given program. For example, to learn about counting words in a file with wc, run:

```
→ man wc
```

To search for manpages by keyword for a particular topic, use the -k option followed by the keyword (shown here piped into the command less to display the results one screenful at a time; press the space bar to continue and q to quit):

```
→ man -k database | less
```

Run the info *command*

The info command is an extended, hypertext help system covering many Linux programs.

```
→ info ls
```

While info is running, some useful keystrokes are:

- To get help, type h
- To quit, type q
- To page forward and backward, use the space bar and Backspace key, respectively
- To jump between hyperlinks, press Tab
- To follow a hyperlink, press Enter

If info has no documentation on a given program, it displays the program's manpage. For a listing of available documentation, type info by itself. To learn how to navigate the info system, type info info.

Use the --help *option (if any)*

Many Linux commands respond to the option --help by printing a short help message. Try:

```
→ wc --help
```

If the output is longer than the screen, pipe it into the less program to display it in pages (press q to quit):

```
→ wc --help | less
```

Examine the directory /usr/share/doc

This directory contains supporting documents for many programs, usually organized by program name and version. For example, files for the text editor emacs, version 24, are likely found (depending on distro) in */usr/share/doc/emacs24*.

Distro-specific websites

Most Linux distros have an official site that includes documentation, discussion forums for questions and answers, and other resources. Simply enter your distro name (e.g., "Ubuntu") into any popular search engine to find its website.

Linux help sites

There are many websites that answer Linux questions, including *http://www.linuxquestions.org*, *http://unix.stackexchange.com*, *http://www.linuxhelp.net*, and *http://www.linuxforums.org*.

Web search

To decipher a specific Linux error message, copy and paste the message into a web search engine, verbatim, and you will likely find helpful results.

Linux: A First View

Linux has four major parts:

The kernel

The low-level operating system, handling files, disks, networking, and other necessities we take for granted. Most users rarely notice the kernel.

Supplied programs

Thousands of programs for file manipulation, text editing, mathematics, web browsing, audio, video, computer programming, typesetting, encryption, DVD burning…you name it.

The shell

A user interface for typing commands, executing them, and displaying the results. Linux has various shells: the Bourne shell, Korn shell, C shell, and others. This book focuses on bash, the Bourne-Again Shell, which is often the default for user accounts. However, all these shells have similar basic functions.

X

A graphical system that provides windows, menus, icons, mouse support, and other familiar GUI elements. More complex graphical environments are built on X; the most popular are KDE and GNOME. We'll discuss only a few programs that open X windows to run.

This book focuses on the second and third parts: supplied programs and the shell.

Running a Shell

If you connect to a Linux machine over a network, you will immediately see a shell, waiting for you to type a command. If instead, you sit down in front of a Linux machine and log into it directly, you're more likely to be greeted by a graphical desktop full of icons and menus, with no shell in sight. For many users, this is the primary way to work with Linux, and those icons and menus are fine for simple tasks such as reading email and browsing the Web. Nevertheless, for the true power of Linux, you must dive beneath this graphical interface, into the shell. It might initially be more difficult than icons and menus, but once you're accustomed to it, the shell becomes easy to use and is *very* powerful.

So, how do you run a shell within this graphical interface? The answer is "it depends." Linux has several graphical interfaces, the most common being GNOME and KDE, and every Linux system may configure them differently! It's your job to locate an icon or menu item that lets you open a *shell window*: a window with a shell running in it. Look in your system's main menu or start menu for an application called Terminal, Konsole, xterm, gnome-terminal, uxterm, or something similar. Launch this program to open a shell window.

The window program (Terminal, Konsole, etc.) is not the shell. It's just a graphical program—possibly with fancy features of its own—that runs a shell on your behalf. The shell is what prompts you for commands and runs them. Figure 2 illustrates this difference.

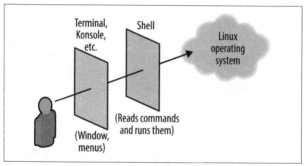

Figure 2. The difference between a shell window and the shell

This was just a quick introduction. We'll discuss additional details in "Shell Features" on page 26, and cover more powerful constructs in "Programming with Shell Scripts" on page 239.

Input and Output

Most Linux commands accept input and produce output. For example, the wc command accepts input from a file and produces output (the number of lines, words, and characters) on the screen.

Linux commands are very flexible with input and output. Input can come from files or from *standard input*, which is usually your keyboard. Likewise, output is written to files or to *standard output*, which is usually your shell window or screen. Error messages are treated specially and displayed on *standard error*, which also is usually your screen but kept separate from standard output.[2] Later, we'll see how to *redirect* standard input, output, and error to and from files or pipes. But let's get our vocabulary straight. When we say a command "reads," we mean from standard input unless we say otherwise. And when a command "writes" or "prints," we mean on standard output, unless we're talking about computer printers.

Users and Superusers

Linux is a multiuser operating system: multiple people can use a single Linux computer at the same time. On a given computer, each user is identified by a *username*, like "smith" or "funkyguy," and owns a (reasonably) private part of the system for doing work.

There is also a special user named *root*—the *superuser*—who has the privileges to do anything at all on the system. Ordinary users are restricted: though they can run most programs, in general they can modify only the files they own. The superuser, on the other hand, can create, modify, or delete any file and run any program; we'll discuss this more in "Becoming the Superuser" on page 170.

---

2 For example, you can capture standard output in a file and still have standard error messages appear on screen.

The Filesystem

To make use of any Linux system, you need to be comfortable with Linux files and *directories* (a.k.a. folders). In a "windows and icons" system, the files and directories are obvious on screen. With a command-line system like the Linux shell, the same files and directories are still present but are not constantly visible, so at times you must remember which directory you are "in" and how it relates to other directories. You'll use shell commands like cd and pwd to "move" between directories and keep track of where you are.

Let's cover some terminology. As we've said, Linux files are collected into directories. The directories form a hierarchy, or *tree*, as in Figure 3: one directory may contain other directories, called *subdirectories*, which may themselves contain other files and subdirectories, and so on, into infinity. The topmost directory is called the *root directory* and is denoted by a slash (/).[3]

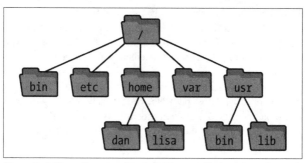

Figure 3. A Linux filesystem (partial). The root directory is at the top. The absolute path to the "dan" directory is /home/dan.

---

3 In Linux, *all* files and directories descend from the root. This is unlike Windows or DOS, in which different devices are accessed by drive letters.

We refer to files and directories using a "names and slashes" syntax called a *path*. For instance, this path:

```
/one/two/three/four
```

refers to the root directory /, which contains a directory called *one*, which contains a directory *two*, which contains a directory *three*, which contains a final file or directory, *four*. Any such path that begins with a slash, which descends all the way from the root, is called an *absolute* path.

Paths don't have to be absolute: they can be relative to some directory other than the root. In Figure 3, there are two different directories named *bin*, whose absolute paths are */bin* and */usr/bin*. If we simply refer to "the *bin* directory," it's not clear which one we mean (and there could be many other *bin* directories too). More context is needed. Any time you refer to a path that doesn't begin with a slash, like *bin*, it's called a *relative* path.

To make sense of a relative path, you need to know "where you are" in the Linux filesystem. This location is called your *current working directory* (or just "current directory"). Every shell has a current working directory, and when you run commands in that shell, they operate relative to that directory. For example, if your shell is "in" the directory */usr*, and you run a command that refers to a relative path *bin*, you're really referring to */usr/bin*. In general, if your current directory is */one/two/three*, a relative path *a/b/c* would imply the absolute path */one/two/three/a/b/c*.

Two special relative paths are denoted . (a single period) and .. (two periods in a row). The former means your current directory, and the latter means your *parent* directory, one level above. So if your current directory is */one/two/three*, then . refers to this directory and .. refers to */one/two*.

You "move" your shell from one directory to another using the cd command:

→ **cd /usr/local/bin**

More technically, this command changes your shell's current working directory to be *_/usr/local/bin_*. This is an absolute change (because the directory begins with "/"). Assuming you installed the book's directory of examples in your home directory, you can jump into it at any time by running:

→ **cd ~/linuxpocketguide**

(where the tilde is a shorthand we'll cover in the next section). You can make relative moves with cd as well:

→ **cd d**   *Enter subdirectory* **d**
→ **cd ../mydir** *Go up to my parent, then into directory mydir*

File and directory names may contain most characters you expect: capital and lowercase letters,[4] numbers, periods, dashes, underscores, and most symbols (but not "/", which is reserved for separating directories). For practical use, however, avoid spaces, asterisks, dollar signs, parentheses, and other characters that have special meaning to the shell. Otherwise, you'll need to quote or escape these characters all the time. (See "Quoting" on page 36.)

Home Directories

Users' personal files are often found in the directory *_/home_* (for ordinary users) or *_/root_* (for the superuser). Your home directory is typically *_/home/<your-username>_* (*_/home/smith_*, *_/home/ jones_*, etc.). There are several ways to locate or refer to your home directory:

---

4 Linux filenames are case-sensitive, so capital and lowercase letters are not equivalent.

cd

> With no arguments, the cd command returns you (i.e., sets the shell's working directory) to your home directory.

HOME *variable*

> The environment variable HOME (see "Shell variables" on page 30) contains the name of your home directory:

> ```
> → echo $HOME        The echo command prints its arguments
> /home/smith
> ```

~

> When used in place of a directory, a lone tilde is expanded by the shell to the name of your home directory.

> ```
> → echo ~
> /home/smith
> ```

> When the tilde is followed by a slash, the path is relative to HOME:

> ```
> → echo ~/linuxpocketguide
> /home/smith/linuxpocketguide
> ```

> When the tilde is followed by a username (as in ~*fred*), the shell expands this string to be the user's home directory:

> ```
> → cd ~fred          If there's a user "fred" on your system
> → pwd               The "print working directory" command
> /home/fred
> ```

System Directories

A typical Linux system has tens of thousands of system directories. These directories contain operating system files, applications, documentation, and just about everything *except* personal user files (which typically live in */home*).

Unless you're a system administrator, you'll rarely visit most system directories—but with a little knowledge you can understand or guess their purposes. Their names often contain three parts, as shown in Figure 4.

/usr/local/share/emacs

Scope · Category · Application

Figure 4. Directory scope, category, and application

Directory path part 1: category

A *category* tells you the types of files found in a directory. For example, if the category is *bin*, you can be reasonably assured that the directory contains programs. Some common categories are as follows:

Categories for programs

bin	Programs (usually binary files)
sbin	Programs (usually binary files) intended to be run by the superuser
lib	Libraries of code used by programs

Categories for documentation

doc	Documentation
info	Documentation files for emacs's built-in help system
man	Documentation files (manual pages) displayed by the man program; the files are often compressed and are sprinkled with typesetting commands for man to interpret
share	Program-specific files, such as examples and installation instructions

Categories for configuration

etc	Configuration files for the system (and other miscellaneous stuff)
init.d	Configuration files for booting Linux
rc.d	Configuration files for booting Linux; also *rc1.d*, *rc2.d*, ...

Categories for programming

include	Header files for programming

src   Source code for programs

Categories for web files

cgi-bin   Scripts/programs that run on web pages

html   Web pages

public_html Web pages, typically in users' home directories

www   Web pages

Categories for display

fonts   Fonts (surprise!)

X11   X window system files

Categories for hardware

dev   Device files for interfacing with disks and other hardware

media   Mount points: directories that provide access to disks

mnt   Mount points: directories that provide access to disks

Categories for runtime files

var   Files specific to this computer, created and updated as the
               computer runs

lock   Lock files, created by programs to say, "I am running"; the
               existence of a lock file may prevent another program, or another
               instance of the same program, from running or performing an
               action

log   Log files that track important system events, containing error,
               warning, and informational messages

mail   Mailboxes for incoming mail

run   PID files, which contain the IDs of running processes; these files are
               often consulted to track or kill particular processes

spool   Files queued or in transit, such as outgoing email, print jobs, and
               scheduled jobs

| *tmp* | Temporary storage for programs and/or people to use |
| *proc* | Operating system state: see "Operating System Directories" on page 24 |

Directory path part 2: scope

The *scope* of a directory path describes, at a high level, the purpose of an entire directory hierarchy. Some common ones are:

/	System files supplied with Linux (pronounced "root")
/usr	More system files supplied with Linux (pronounced "user")
/usr/local	System files developed "locally," either for your organization or your individual computer
/usr/games	Games (surprise!)

So for a category like *lib* (libraries), your Linux system might have directories */lib*, */usr/lib*, */usr/local/lib*, and */usr/games/lib*.

There isn't a clear distinction between / and */usr* in practice, but there is a sense that / is "lower level" and closer to the operating system. So */bin* contains more fundamental programs than */usr/bin* does, such as ls and cat, and */lib* contains more fundamental libraries than */usr/lib* does, and so on.[5] */usr/local/bin* contains programs not included in your distro. These are not hard-and-fast rules but typical cases.

Directory path part 3: application

The application part of a directory path, if present, is usually the name of a program. After the scope and category (say, */usr/local/doc*), a program may have its own subdirectory (say, */usr/local/doc/myprogram*) containing files it needs.

---

5 Some distros no longer make these distinctions. Fedora, for example, makes */bin* a symbolic link to */usr/bin*.

Operating System Directories

Some directories support the Linux kernel, the lowest-level part of the Linux operating system:

/boot

Files for booting the system. This is where the kernel lives, typically named */boot/vmlinuz* or similar.

/lost+found

Damaged files that were rescued by a disk recovery tool.

/proc

Describes currently running processes; for advanced users.

The files in */proc* provide views into the running kernel and have special properties. They always appear to be zero sized, read-only, and dated now:

```
→ ls -lG /proc/version
-r--r--r-- 1 root  0 Oct  3 22:55 /proc/version
```

However, their contents magically contain information about the Linux kernel:

```
→ cat /proc/version
Linux version 2.6.32-71.el6.i686 ...
```

Files in */proc* are used mostly by programs, but feel free to explore them. Here are some examples:

/proc/ ioports	A list of your computer's input/output hardware.
/proc/ cpuinfo	Information about your computer's processors.
/proc/ version	The operating system version. The uname command prints the same information.
/proc/ uptime	System uptime (i.e., seconds elapsed since the system was last booted). Run the uptime command for a more human-readable result.

| */proc/nnn* | Information about the Linux process with ID *nnn*, where *nnn* is a positive integer. |
| */proc/self* | Information about the current process you're running; a symbolic link to a */proc/nnn* file, automatically updated. Try running: |

      → `ls -l /proc/self`

several times in a row: you'll see */proc/self* changing where it points.

File Protections

A Linux system may have many users with login accounts. To maintain privacy and security, most users can access only *some* files on the system, not all. This access control is embodied in two questions:

Who has permission?

Every file and directory has an *owner* who has permission to do anything with it. Typically, the user who created a file is its owner, but ownership can be changed by the superuser.

Additionally, a predefined *group* of users may have permission to access a file. Groups are defined by the system administrator and are covered in "Group Management" on page 172.

Finally, a file or directory can be opened to *all users* with login accounts on the system. You'll also see this set of users called *the world* or simply *other*.

What kind of permission is granted?

File owners, groups, and the world may each have permission to *read*, *write* (modify), and *execute* (run) particular files. Permissions also extend to directories, which users may read (access files within the directory), write (create and delete files within the directory), and execute (enter the directory with cd).

To see the ownership and permissions of a file named *myfile*, run:

```
→ ls -l myfile
-rw-r--r-- 1 smith smith  1168 Oct 28  2015 myfile
```

To see the ownership and permissions of a directory named *mydir*, add the -d option:

```
→ ls -ld mydir
drwxr-x--- 3 smith smith  4096 Jan 08 15:02 mydir
```

In the output, the file permissions are the 10 leftmost characters, a string of r (read), w (write), x (execute), other letters, and dashes. For example:

```
-rwxr-x---
```

Here's what these letters and symbols mean:

Position	Meaning
1	File type: - = file, d = directory, l = symbolic link, p = named pipe, c = character device, b = block device
2–4	Read, write, and execute permissions for the file's owner
5–7	Read, write, and execute permissions for the file's group
8–10	Read, write, and execute permissions for all other users

So our example -rwxr-x--- means a file that can be read, written, and executed by the owner, read and executed by the group, and not accessed at all by other users. We describe ls in more detail in "Basic File Operations" on page 47. To change the owner, group ownership, or permissions of a file, use the chown, chgrp, and chmod commands, respectively, as described in "File Properties" on page 69.

Shell Features

In order to run commands on a Linux system, you'll need somewhere to type them. That "somewhere" is called the *shell*, which is Linux's command-line user interface: you type a command and press Enter, and the shell runs whatever program (or programs) you've requested. (See "Running a Shell" on page 14 to learn how to open a shell window.)

For example, to see who's logged into the computer, you could execute this command in a shell:

```
→ who
silver      :0      Sep 23 20:44
byrnes     pts/0    Sep 15 13:51
barrett    pts/1    Sep 22 21:15
silver     pts/2    Sep 22 21:18
```

(Recall that the → symbol represents the shell prompt for us, indicating that the shell is ready to run a command.) A single command can also invoke several programs at the same time, and even connect programs together so they interact. Here's a command that redirects the output of the who program to become the input of the wc program, which counts lines of text in a file; the result is the number of lines in the output of who:

```
→ who | wc -l
4
```

telling you how many users are logged in.[6] The vertical bar, called a *pipe*, makes the connection between who and wc.

A shell is actually a program itself, and Linux has several. We focus on bash (the Bourne-Again Shell), located in */bin/bash*, which is usually the default in Linux distros. To see if you're running bash, type:

```
→ echo $SHELL
/bin/bash
```

If you're not running bash and wish to do so, you can run the command bash directly (type exit when done to return to your

---

6 Actually, how many interactive shells those users are running. If a user has two shells running, like the user "silver" in our example, he'll have two lines of output from who.

regular shell). To make bash your default shell, see chsh on page 170.

The Shell Versus Programs

When you run a command, it might invoke a Linux program (like who), or instead it might be a *built-in command*, a feature of the shell itself. You can tell the difference with the type command:

```
→ type who
who is /usr/bin/who
→ type cd
cd is a shell builtin
```

Selected Features of the bash Shell

A shell does much more than simply run commands. It also has powerful features to make this task easier: wildcards for matching filenames, a "command history" to recall previous commands quickly, pipes for making the output of one command become the input of another, variables for storing values for use by the shell, and more. Take the time to learn these features, and you will become faster and more productive with Linux. Let's skim the surface and introduce you to these useful tools. (For full documentation, run info bash.)

Wildcards

Wildcards are a shorthand for sets of files with similar names. For example, a* means all files whose names begin with lower-case "a". Wildcards are "expanded" by the shell into the actual set of filenames they match. So if you type:

```
→ ls a*
```

the shell first expands a* into the filenames that begin with "a" in your current directory, as if you had typed:

```
→ ls aardvark adamantium apple
```

ls never knows you used a wildcard: it sees only the final list of filenames after the shell expands the wildcard. This means *every* Linux command, regardless of its origin, works with wildcards and other shell features. This is a critically important point. A surprising number of Linux users mistakenly think that programs expand their own wildcards. They don't. Wildcards are handled completely by the shell before the associated program even runs.

Dot Files

Filenames with a leading period, called *dot files*, are special in Linux. When you name a file beginning with a period, it will not be displayed by some programs:

- ls will omit the file from directory listings, unless you provide the -a option.
- Shell wildcards do not match a leading period.

Effectively, dot files are hidden unless you explicitly ask to see them. As a result, sometimes they are called "hidden files."

Wildcards never match two characters: a leading period, and the directory slash (/). These must be given literally, as in .pro* to match *.profile*, or /etc/*conf to match all filenames ending in *conf* in the */etc* directory.

Wildcard	Meaning
*	Zero or more consecutive characters
?	Any single character
[set]	Any single character in the given *set*, most commonly a sequence of characters, like [aeiouAEIOU] for all vowels, or a range with a dash, like [A-Z] for all capital letters
[^set]	Any single character *not* in the given *set*, such as [^0-9] to mean any nondigit

Wildcard	Meaning
[!*set*]	Same as [^*set*]

When using character sets, if you want to include a literal dash in the set, put it first or last. To include a literal closing square bracket in the set, put it first. To include a ^ or ! symbol literally, don't put it first.

Brace expansion

Similar to wildcards, expressions with curly braces also expand to become multiple arguments to a command. The comma-separated expression:

```
{X,YY,ZZZ}
```

expands first to X, then YY, and finally ZZZ within a command line, like this:

```
→ echo sand{X,YY,ZZZ}wich
sandXwich sandYYwich sandZZZwich
```

Braces work with any strings, unlike wildcards which expand only if they match existing filenames.

Shell variables

You can define variables and their values by assigning them:

```
→ MYVAR=3
```

To refer to a value, simply place a dollar sign in front of the variable name:

```
→ echo $MYVAR
3
```

Some variables are standard and commonly defined by your shell upon login:

Variable	Meaning
DISPLAY	The name of your X window display
HOME	Your home directory, such as /home/smith
LOGNAME	Your login name, such as smith
MAIL	Your incoming mailbox, such as /var/spool/mail/smith
OLDPWD	Your shell's previous directory, prior to the last cd command
PATH	Your shell search path: directories separated by colons
PWD	Your shell's current directory
SHELL	The path to your shell (e.g., /bin/bash)
TERM	The type of your terminal (e.g., xterm or vt100)
USER	Your login name

The scope of the variable (i.e., which programs know about it) is, by default, the shell in which it's defined. To make a variable and its value available to other programs your shell invokes (i.e., subshells), use the export command:

→ **export MYVAR**

or the shorthand:

→ **export MYVAR=3**

Your variable is now called an *environment variable*, because it's available to other programs in your shell's "environment." So in the preceding example, the exported variable MYVAR is available to all programs run by that same shell (including shell scripts: see "Variables" on page 241).

To list a shell's environment variables, run:

→ **printenv**

To provide the value of an environment variable to a specific program just once, prepend *variable=value* to the command line:

```
→ printenv HOME
/home/smith
→ HOME=/home/sally printenv HOME
/home/sally
→ printenv HOME
/home/smith          The original value is unaffected
```

Search path

Programs are scattered all over the Linux filesystem, in directories like */bin* and */usr/bin*. When you run a program via a shell command, how does the shell find it? The critical variable PATH tells the shell where to look. When you type any command:

```
→ who
```

the shell locates the who program by searching through Linux directories. The shell consults the value of PATH, which is a sequence of directories separated by colons:

```
→ echo $PATH
/usr/local/bin:/bin:/usr/bin
```

and looks for the who command in each of these directories. If it finds who (say, */usr/bin/who*), it runs the command. Otherwise, it reports a failure such as:

```
bash: who: command not found
```

To add directories to your shell's search path temporarily, modify its PATH variable. For example, to append */usr/sbin* to your shell's search path:

```
→ PATH=$PATH:/usr/sbin
→ echo $PATH
/usr/local/bin:/bin:/usr/bin:/usr/sbin
```

This change affects only the current shell. To make it permanent, modify the PATH variable in your startup file *~/.bash_pro-*

file, as explained in "Tailoring Shell Behavior" on page 46. Then log out and log back in, or run your *~/.bash_profile* startup file by hand in each of your open shell windows with:

```
→ . $HOME/.bash_profile
```

Aliases

The built-in command `alias` defines a convenient shorthand for a longer command, to save typing. For example:

```
→ alias ll='ls -lG'
```

defines a new command `ll` that runs `ls -lG`:

```
→ ll
total 436
-rw-r--r--    1 smith    3584 Oct 11 14:59 file1
-rwxr-xr-x    1 smith      72 Aug  6 23:04 file2
...
```

Define aliases in your *~/.bash_aliases* file (see "Tailoring Shell Behavior" on page 46) to be available whenever you log in.[7] To list all your aliases, type `alias`. If aliases don't seem powerful enough for you (because they have no parameters or branching), see "Programming with Shell Scripts" on page 239, run `info bash`, and read up on "shell functions."

Input/output redirection

The shell can redirect standard input, standard output, and standard error (see "Input and Output" on page 15) to and from files. In other words, any command that reads from standard input can have its input come from a file instead with the shell's < operator:

```
→ any command < infile
```

---

7 Some setups use *~/.bashrc* for this purpose.

Likewise, any command that writes to standard output can write to a file instead:

→ *any command* **> outfile**   *Create/overwrite outfile*
→ *any command* **>> outfile**   *Append to outfile*

A command that writes to standard error can have its output redirected to a file as well, while standard output still goes to the screen:

→ *any command* **2> errorfile**

To redirect both standard output and standard error to files:

→ *any command* **> outfile 2> errorfile**   *Separate files*
→ *any command* **>& outfile**   *Single file*
→ *any command* **&> outfile**   *Single file*

Pipes

You can redirect the standard output of one command to be the standard input of another, using the shell's pipe (|) operator. (On US keyboards, you can find this symbol just above the Enter key.) For example:

→ **who | sort**

sends the output of who into the sort program, printing an alphabetically sorted list of logged-in users. Multiple pipes work too. Here we sort the output of who again, extract the first column of information (using awk), and display the results one page at a time (using less):

→ **who | sort | awk '{print $1}' | less**

Process substitution

Pipes let you send one program's output to another program. A more advanced feature, process substitution, lets that output masquerade as a *named* file. Consider a program that compares the contents of two files. With the process substitution operator, <( ), you can compare the outputs of two programs instead.

Suppose you have a directory full of JPEG and text files in pairs:

```
→ ls jpegexample
file1.jpg  file1.txt  file2.jpg  file2.txt ...
```

and you want to confirm that every JPEG file has a corresponding text file and vice versa. Ordinarily, you might create two temporary files, one containing the JPEG filenames and the other containing the text filenames, remove the file extensions with cut, and compare the two temporary files with diff:

```
→ cd jpegexample
→ ls *.jpg | cut -d. -f1 > /tmp/jpegs
→ ls *.txt | cut -d. -f1 > /tmp/texts
→ diff /tmp/jpegs /tmp/texts
5a6
> file6          No file6.jpg was found
8d8
< file9          No file9.txt was found
```

With process substitution, you can perform the same task with a single command and no temporary files:

```
→ diff <(ls *.jpg|cut -d. -f1) <(ls *.txt|cut -d. -f1)
```

Each <() operator stands in for a filename on the command line, as if that "file" contained the output of ls and cut.

Combining commands

To invoke several commands in sequence on a single command line, separate them with semicolons:

```
→ command1 ; command2 ; command3
```

To run a sequence of commands as before, but stop execution if any of them fails, separate them with && ("and") symbols:

```
→ command1 && command2 && command3
```

To run a sequence of commands, stopping execution as soon as one succeeds, separate them with `||` ("or") symbols:

```
→ command1 || command2 || command3
```

Quoting

Normally, the shell treats whitespace simply as separating the words on the command line. If you want a word to *contain* whitespace (e.g., a filename with a space in it), surround it with single or double quotes to make the shell treat it as a unit. Single quotes treat their contents literally, while double quotes let shell constructs be evaluated, such as variables:

```
→ echo 'The variable HOME has value $HOME'
The variable HOME has value $HOME
→ echo "The variable HOME has value $HOME"
The variable HOME has value /home/smith
```

Backquotes ("backticks") cause their contents to be evaluated as a shell command. The contents are then replaced by the standard output of the command:

```
→ date +%Y              Print the current year
2016
→ echo This year is `date +%Y`
This year is 2016
```

A dollar sign and parentheses are equivalent to backquotes:

```
→ echo This year is $(date +%Y)
This year is 2016
```

but are superior because they can be nested:

```
→ echo Next year is $(expr $(date +%Y) + 1)
Next year is 2017
```

Escaping

If a character has special meaning to the shell but you want it used literally (e.g., `*` as a literal asterisk rather than a wildcard), precede the character with the backward slash "\" character. This is called *escaping* the special character:

```
→ echo a*          As a wildcard, matching "a" filenames
aardvark  adamantium  apple
→ echo a\*                      As a literal asterisk
a*
→ echo "I live in $HOME"     Print a variable value
I live in /home/smith
→ echo "I live in \$HOME"     A literal dollar sign
I live in $HOME
```

You can also escape control characters (tabs, newlines, ^D, etc.) to have them used literally on the command line, if you precede them with ^V. This is particularly useful for tab characters, which the shell would otherwise use for filename completion (see "Filename completion" on page 39).

```
→ echo "There is a tab between here^V    and here"
There is a tab between here    and here
```

Command-line editing

Bash lets you edit the command line you're working on, using keystrokes inspired by the text editors emacs and vi (see "File Creation and Editing" on page 63). To enable command-line editing with emacs keys, run this command (and place it in your ~/.bash_profile to make it permanent):

```
→ set -o emacs
```

For vi (or vim) keys:

```
→ set -o vi
```

emacs keystroke	vi keystroke (after ESC)	Meaning
^P or up arrow	k	Go to previous command
^N or down arrow	j	Go to next command

emacs keystroke	vi keystroke (after ESC)	Meaning
^R		Search for a previous command interactively
^F or right arrow	l	Go forward one character
^B or left arrow	h	Go backward one character
^A	0	Go to beginning of line
^E	$	Go to end of line
^D	x	Delete next character
^U	^U	Erase entire line

Command history

You can recall previous commands you've run—that is, the shell's *history*—and re-execute them. Some useful history-related commands are listed here:

Command	Meaning
history	Print your history
history N	Print the most recent N commands in your history
history -c	Clear (delete) your history
!!	Re-run previous command
!N	Re-run command number N in your history
!-N	Re-run the command you typed N commands ago
!$	Represents the last parameter from the previous command; great for checking that files are present before running a destructive operation, like removing them: → ls z* zebra.txt zookeeper → rm !$ *Same as "rm z*"*

Command	Meaning
!*	Represents all parameters from the previous command:

```
→ ls myfile emptyfile hugefile
emptyfile  hugefile  myfile
→ wc !*
     18      211      1168 myfile
      0        0         0 emptyfile
 333563  2737539  18577838 hugefile
 333581  2737750  18579006 total
```

Filename completion

Press the Tab key while you are in the middle of typing a file-name, and the shell will automatically complete (finish typing) the filename for you. If several filenames match what you've typed so far, the shell will beep, indicating the match is ambiguous. Immediately press Tab again and the shell will present the alternatives. Try this:

```
→ cd /usr/bin
→ ls un<Tab><Tab>
```

The shell will display all files in */usr/bin* that begin with *un*, such as *uniq* and *unzip*. Type a few more characters to disambiguate your choice and press Tab again.

Shell Job Control

jobs	List your jobs.
&	Run a job in the background.
^Z	Suspend the current (foreground) job.
suspend	Suspend a shell.
fg	Unsuspend a job: bring it into the foreground.
bg	Make a suspended job run in the background.

All Linux shells have *job control*: the ability to run commands in the background (multitasking behind the scenes) and foreground (running as the active process at your shell prompt). A *job* is simply the shell's unit of work. When you run a command interactively, your current shell tracks it as a job. When the command completes, the associated job disappears. Jobs are at a higher level than Linux processes; the Linux operating system knows nothing about them. They are merely constructs of the shell. Here is some important vocabulary about job control:

Foreground job
> Running in a shell, occupying the shell prompt so you cannot run another command

Background job
> Running in a shell, but not occupying the shell prompt, so you can run another command in the same shell

Suspend
> To stop a foreground job temporarily

Resume
> To cause a suspended job to start running in the foreground again

---

jobs

The built-in command jobs lists the jobs running in your current shell:

```
→ jobs
[1]-  Running            emacs myfile &
[2]+  Stopped            ssh example.com
```

The integer on the left is the job number, and the plus sign identifies the default job affected by the fg (foreground) and bg (background) commands.

&

Placed at the end of a command line, the ampersand causes the given command to run as a background job:

```
→ emacs myfile &
[2] 28090
```

The shell's response includes the job number (2) and the process ID of the command (28090).

^Z

Typing ^Z in a shell, while a job is running in the foreground, will suspend that job. It simply stops running, but its state is remembered:

```
→ sleep 10           Waits for 10 seconds
^Z
[1]+  Stopped            sleep 10
→
```

Now you're ready to type bg to put the command into the background, or fg to resume it in the foreground. You could also leave it suspended and run other commands.

suspend

The built-in command suspend will suspend the current shell if possible, as if you'd typed ^Z to the shell itself. For instance, if

you've created a superuser shell with the sudo command and
want to return to your original shell:

```
→ whoami
smith
→ sudo bash
Password: *******
# whoami
root
# suspend
[1]+  Stopped                 sudo bash
→ whoami
smith
```

bg

bg [%*jobnumber*]

The built-in command bg sends a suspended job to run in the
background. With no arguments, bg operates on the most
recently suspended job. To specify a particular job (shown by
the jobs command), supply the job number preceded by a percent sign:

```
→ bg %2
```

Some types of interactive jobs cannot remain in the background—for instance, if they are waiting for input. If you try,
the shell will suspend the job and display:

```
[2]+  Stopped         command line here
```

You can now resume the job (with fg) and continue.

fg

```
fg [%jobnumber]
```

The built-in command fg brings a suspended or backgrounded job into the foreground. With no arguments, it selects a job, usually the most recently suspended or backgrounded one. To specify a particular job (as shown by the jobs command), supply the job number preceded by a percent sign:

→ **fg %2**

Running Multiple Shells at Once

Job control lets you manage several commands at once, but only one can run in the foreground at a time. More powerfully, you can also run multiple shells at once, each with a foreground command and any number of background commands.

If your Linux computer runs a window system such as KDE or Gnome, you can easily run many shells at the same time by opening multiple shell windows (see "Running a Shell" on page 14). In addition, certain shell window programs, such as KDE's konsole, can open multiple tabs within a single window, each one running a shell.

Even without a window system—say, over an SSH network connection—you can manage multiple shells at once. The program screen uses an ordinary ASCII terminal to simulate multiple windows, each running a shell. Using special keystrokes, you can switch from one simulated window to another at will. (Another such program is tmux.) To begin a session with screen, simply run:

→ **screen**

You may see some introductory messages, and then your ordinary shell prompt. It looks like nothing has happened, but you're now running a new shell inside a virtual "window." The screen program provides 10 such windows, labeled from 0 to 9.

Type a simple command such as ls, then press ^A^C (control-A, control-C). The screen will clear and show you a fresh shell prompt. You are actually viewing a second, independent "window." Run a different command (say, df), then press ^A^A and you'll switch back to the first window, where your output from ls is now visible again. Press ^A^A a second time to toggle back to the second window. Some other common keystrokes for screen are listed here (see the manpage or type ^A? for on-screen help):

^A?	Help: show all keystroke commands.
^A^C	Create a window.
^A0, ^A1 ... ^A9	Switch to window 0 through 9, respectively.
^A'	Prompt for a window number (0–9) and then switch to it.
^A^N	Switch to the next window, numerically.
^A^P	Switch to the previous window, numerically.
^A^A	Switch to the other window you've used most recently (toggling between two windows).
^A^W	List all your windows.
^AN	Display the current window number. (Note that the N is capitalized.)
^Aa	Send a true control-A to your shell, ignored by screen. In bash, control-A normally moves the cursor to the beginning of the command line. (Note that the second a is lowercase.)
^D	Terminate the current shell. This is the ordinary "end of file" keystroke, explained in "Terminating a Shell" on page 46, which closes any shell.
^A\	Kill all windows and terminate screen.

Beware when running a text editor in a screen window. screen will capture all your control-A keystrokes, even if they are intended as editing commands. Type ^Aa to send a true control-A to your application.

Killing a Command in Progress

If you've launched a command from the shell running in the foreground, and want to kill it immediately, type ^C. The shell recognizes ^C as meaning, "terminate the current foreground command right now." So if you are displaying a very long file (say, with the cat command) and want to stop, type ^C:

```
→ cat hugefile
Lorem ipsum dolor sit amet, consectetur adipiscing
odio. Praesent libero. Sed cursus ante dapibus diam.
quis sem at nibh elementum blah blah blah ^C
→
```

To kill a program running in the background, you can bring it into the foreground with fg and then type ^C:

```
→ sleep 50 &
[1] 12752
→ jobs
[1]-  Running        sleep 50 &
→ fg %1
sleep 50
^C
→
```

or alternatively, use the kill command (see "Controlling Processes" on page 147).

Surviving a Kill

Killing a foreground program with ^C may leave your shell in an odd or unresponsive state, perhaps not displaying the keystrokes you type. This happens because the killed program had no opportunity to clean up after itself. If this happens to you:

---

1. Press ^J to get a shell prompt. This keystroke produces the same character as the Enter key (a newline) but will work even if Enter does not.

2. Type the shell command reset (even if the letters don't appear while you type) and press ^J again to run this command. This should bring your shell back to normal.

Typing ^C is not a friendly way to end a program. If the program has its own way to exit, use that when possible (refer to the preceding sidebar for details).

^C works only within a shell. It will likely have no effect if typed in an application that is not a shell window. Additionally, some command-line programs are written to "catch" the ^C and ignore it: an example is the text editor emacs.

Terminating a Shell

To terminate a shell, either run the exit command or type ^D.[8]

→ **exit**

Tailoring Shell Behavior

To configure all your shells to work in a particular way, edit the files *.bash_profile* and *.bashrc* in your home directory. These files execute each time you log in (*~/.bash_profile*) or open a shell (*~/.bashrc*). They can set variables and aliases, run programs, print your horoscope, or whatever you like.

These two files are examples of *shell scripts*: executable files that contain shell commands. We'll cover this feature in more detail in "Programming with Shell Scripts" on page 239.

---

8 Control-D sends an "end of file" signal to any program reading from standard input. In this case, the program is the shell itself, which terminates.

This concludes our basic overview of Linux and the shell. Now we turn to Linux commands, listing and describing the most useful commands for working with files, processes, users, networking, multimedia, and more.

Basic File Operations

ls   List files in a directory.

cp   Copy a file.

mv   Rename ("move") a file.

rm   Delete ("remove") a file.

ln   Create links (alternative names) to a file.

One of the first things you'll need to do on a Linux system is manipulate files: copying, renaming, deleting, and so forth.

---

ls   stdin   **stdout**   - file   -- opt   **--help**   **--version**

ls [*options*] [*files*]

The ls command (pronounced as it is spelled, *ell ess*) lists attributes of files and directories. You can list files in the current directory:

→ **ls**

in given directories:

→ **ls dir1 dir2 dir3**

or individually:

→ **ls myfile myfile2 myfile3**

The most important options are -a, -l, and -d. By default, ls hides files whose names begin with a dot, as explained in the sidebar "Dot Files" on page 29. The -a option displays all files:

```
→ ls
myfile    myfile2
→ ls -a
.hidden_file    myfile    myfile2
```

The -l option produces a long listing:

```
→ ls -l myfile
-rw-r--r--  1 smith users  1168 Oct 28 2015 myfile
```

that includes, from left to right: the file's permissions (-rw-r--r--), number of hard links (1), owner (smith), group (users), size (1168 bytes), last modification date (Oct 28 2015) and name. See "File Protections" on page 25 for more information on permissions.

The -d option lists information about a directory itself, rather than descending into the directory to list its files:

```
→ ls -ld dir1
drwxr-xr-x  1 smith users  4096 Oct 29 2015 dir1
```

Useful options

- -a List all files, including those whose names begin with a dot.

- -l Long listing, including file attributes. Add the -h option (human-readable) to print file sizes in kilobytes, megabytes, and gigabytes, instead of bytes.

- -G In a long listing, don't print the group ownership of the file.

- -F Decorate certain filenames with meaningful symbols, indicating their types. Appends "/" to directories, "*" to executables, "@" to symbolic links, "|" to named pipes, and "=" to sockets. These are just visual indicators for you, not part of the filenames!

- -S Sort files by their size.

- -t Sort files by the time they were last modified.

- -r Reverse the sorted order.

- -R If listing a directory, list its contents recursively.

- -d If listing a directory, do not list its contents, just the directory itself.

cp [*options*] *files* (*file* | *directory*)

The cp command normally copies a file:

→ **cp myfile anotherfile**

or copies multiple files into a directory (say) *mydir*:

→ **cp myfile myfile2 myfile3 mydir**

Using the -a or -r option, you can also recursively copy directories.

Useful options

- -p   Copy not only the file contents, but also the file's permissions, timestamps, and if you have sufficient permission to do so, its owner and group. (Normally the copies will be owned by you, timestamped now, with permissions set by applying your umask to the original permissions.)

- -a   Copy a directory hierarchy recursively, preserving all file attributes and links.

- -r   Copy a directory hierarchy recursively. This option does not preserve the files' attributes such as permissions and timestamps. It does preserve symbolic links.

- -i   Interactive mode. Ask before overwriting destination files.

- -f   Force the copy. If a destination file exists, overwrite it unconditionally.

mv [*options*] *source target*

The mv (move) command can rename a file:

→ **mv somefile yetanotherfile**

or move files and directories into a destination directory:

→ `mv myfile myfile2 dir1 dir2 destination_directory`

Useful options

- `-i` Interactive mode. Ask before overwriting destination files.

- `-f` Force the move. If a destination file exists, overwrite it unconditionally.

---

rm   stdin   stdout   -file   --opt   --help   --version

`rm [options] files | directories`

The `rm` (remove) command can delete files:

→ `rm deleteme deleteme2`

or recursively delete directories:

→ `rm -r dir1 dir2`

Useful options

- `-i` Interactive mode. Ask before deleting each file.

- `-f` Force the deletion, ignoring any errors or warnings.

- `-r` Recursively remove a directory and its contents. Use with caution, especially if combined with the `-f` option, as it can wipe out all your files.

---

ln   stdin   stdout   -file   --opt   --help   --version

`ln [options] source target`

A *link* is a reference to another file, created by the `ln` command. Intuitively, links give the same file multiple names, allowing it to live in two (or more) locations at once.

There are two kinds of links. A *symbolic link* (also called a *symlink* or *soft link*) refers to another file by its path, much like a Windows "shortcut" or a Mac OS X "alias." To create a symbolic link, use the -s option:

→ `ln -s myfile mysoftlink`

If you delete the original file, the now-dangling link will be invalid, pointing to a nonexistent file path. A *hard link*, on the other hand, is simply a *second name* for a physical file on disk (in tech talk, it points to the same *inode*). If you delete the original file, the link still works. Figure 5 illustrates the difference. To create a hard link, type:

→ `ln myfile myhardlink`

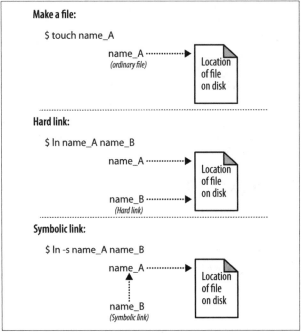

Figure 5. Hard link versus symbolic link

Symbolic links can point to files on other disk partitions, as they are just references to file paths; hard links cannot, because an inode on one disk has no meaning on another. Symbolic links can also point to directories, whereas hard links cannot...unless you are the superuser and use the -d option.

Useful options

- -s   Make a symbolic link instead of a hard link.
- -i   Interactive mode. Ask before overwriting destination files.
- -f   Force the link. If a destination file exists, overwrite it unconditionally.
- -d   Create a hard link to a directory (superusers only).

To find out where a symbolic link points, run either of the following commands, which show that the link *examplelink* points to the file *myfile*:

```
→ readlink examplelink
myfile
→ ls -l examplelink
lrwxrwxrwx 1 smith    ...    examplelink -> myfile
```

Symbolic links can point to other symbolic links. To follow an entire chain of links to discover where they point in the end, use readlink -f.

Directory Operations

cd	Change your current directory (i.e., "where you are now" in the filesystem).
pwd	Print the name of your current directory.
basename	Print the final part of a file path.
dirname	Print a file path without its final part.
mkdir	Create (make) a directory.
rmdir	Delete (remove) an empty directory.

rm -r   Delete a nonempty directory and its contents.

We discussed the directory structure of Linux in "The Filesystem" on page 17. Now we'll cover commands that create, modify, delete, and manipulate directories within that structure.

---

cd   stdin   stdout   - file   -- opt   --help   --version

cd [*directory*]

The cd (change directory) command sets your current working directory:

→ **cd /usr/games**

With no directory supplied, cd defaults to your home directory:

→ **cd**

---

pwd   stdin   **stdout**   - file   -- opt   --help   --version

pwd

The pwd command prints the absolute path of your current working directory:

→ **pwd**
/users/smith/linuxpocketguide

basename   stdin   **stdout**   - file   -- opt   **--help**   **--version**

basename *path* [*extension*]

The basename command prints the final component in a file path:

→ **basename /users/smith/finances/money.txt**
money.txt

If you provide an optional extension, it gets stripped from the result:

→ **basename /users/smith/finances/money.txt .txt**
money

---

dirname   stdin   **stdout**   - file   -- opt   **--help**   **--version**

dirname *path*

The dirname command prints a file path with its final component removed:

→ **dirname /users/smith/mydir**
/users/smith

dirname does not change your current working directory. It simply manipulates and prints a string, just like basename does.

---

mkdir   stdin   stdout   - file   **-- opt**   **--help**   **--version**

mkdir [*options*] *directories*

mkdir creates one or more directories:

→ **mkdir directory1 directory2 directory3**

Useful options

-p	Given a directory path (not just a simple directory name), create any necessary parent directories automatically. The command:

→ mkdir -p one/two/three

creates *one* and *one/two* and *one/two/three* if they don't already exist.

-m	Create the directory with the given permissions:
mode	→ mkdir -m 0755 publicdir

By default, your shell's umask controls the permissions. See the chmod command in "File Properties" on page 69, and "File Protections" on page 25.

---

rmdir

rmdir [*options*] *directories*

The rmdir (remove directory) command deletes one or more empty directories you name:

→ mkdir /tmp/junk   *make a directory*
→ rmdir /tmp/junk

Useful options

-p	If you supply a directory path (not just a simple directory name), delete not only the given directory, but the specified parent directories automatically, all of which must be empty. So rmdir -p one/two/three will delete not only *one/two/three*, but also *one/two* and *one*.

To delete a nonempty directory and its contents, use (carefully) rm -r *directory*. Use rm -ri to delete interactively, or rm -rf to annihilate without any error messages or confirmation.

File Viewing

`cat`	View files in their entirety.
`less`	View text files one page at a time.
`nl`	View text files with their lines numbered.
`head`	View the first lines of a text file.
`tail`	View the last lines of a text file.
`strings`	Display text that's embedded in a binary file.
`od`	View data in octal (or other formats).

In Linux, you'll encounter files that contain readable text, and others that contain binary data that you want to view in a readable manner. Here, we'll demonstrate how to display their contents at the most basic level.

---

cat   **stdin**   **stdout**   **- file**   **-- opt**   **--help**   **--version**

`cat [options] [files]`

The simplest viewer is `cat`, which just prints its files to standard output, concatenating them (hence the name):

→ `cat myfile`

Large files will likely scroll off screen, so consider using `less` if you plan to read the output. That being said, `cat` is particularly useful for sending a set of files into a shell pipeline:

→ `cat myfile* | wc`

`cat` can also manipulate its output in small ways, optionally displaying nonprinting characters, prepending line numbers (though the `nl` command is more powerful for this purpose), and eliminating whitespace.

Useful options

-T   Print tabs as ^I.

-E   Print newlines as $.

-v   Print other nonprinting characters in a human-readable format.

-n   Prepend line numbers to every line.

-b   Prepend line numbers to nonblank lines.

-s   Squeeze each sequence of blank lines into a single blank line.

---

less   stdin   stdout[9]   - file   -- opt   --help   --version

```
less [options] [files]
```

Use less to view text one "page" at a time (i.e., one window or screenful at a time):

→ **less myfile**

It's great for text files, or as the final command in a shell pipeline with lengthy output:

→ *command1* | *command2* | *command3* | *command4* | **less**

While running less, type h for a help message describing all its features. Here are some useful keystrokes for paging through files:

Keystroke	Meaning
h, H	View a help page.
Space bar, f, ^V, ^F	Move forward one screenful.

---

9 Although technically less can be plugged into the middle of a pipeline, or its output redirected to a file, there isn't much point to doing this.

Keystroke	Meaning
Enter	Move forward one line.
b, ^B, ESC-v	Move backward one screenful.
/	Enter search mode. Follow it with a regular expression and press Enter, and less will look for the first matching line.
?	Same as /, but it searches backward in the file.
n	Next match: Repeat your most recent search forward.
N	Repeat your most recent search backward.
v	Edit the current file with your default text editor (the value of environment variable VISUAL, or if not defined, EDITOR, or if not defined, the program vi).
<, g	Jump to beginning of file.
>, G	Jump to end of file.
:n	Jump to next file.
:p	Jump to previous file.

less has a mind-boggling number of features; we're presenting only the most common. (For instance, less will display the contents of a compressed Zip file: try less myfile.zip.) The manpage is recommended reading.

Useful options

- -c   Clear the screen before displaying the next page. This avoids scrolling and may be more comfortable on the eyes.

- -m   Print a more verbose prompt, displaying the percentage of the file displayed so far.

- -N   Display line numbers.

- -r   Display control characters literally; normally less converts them to a human-readable format.

- -s   Squeeze multiple, adjacent blank lines into a single blank line.

- S   Truncate long lines to the width of the screen, instead of wrapping.

---

nl   stdin   stdout   - file   -- opt   --help   --version

nl [*options*] [*files*]

nl copies its files to standard output, prepending line numbers:

→ **nl poem**
        1 Once upon a time, there was
        2 a little operating system named
        3 Linux, which everybody loved.

It's more flexible than cat with its -n and -b options, providing
greater control over the numbering.

Useful options

-b [a|t|n|p R]	Prepend numbers to all lines (a), nonblank lines (t), no lines (n), or only lines that contain regular expression R. (Default=a)
-v N	Begin numbering with integer N. (Default=1)
-i N	Increment the number by N for each line, so for example, you could use odd numbers only (-i2) or even numbers only (-v2 -i2). (Default=1)
-n [ln|rn|rz]	Format numbers as left-justified (ln), right-justified (rn), or right-justified with leading zeros (rz). (Default=ln)
-w N	Force the width of the number to be N columns. (Default=6)
-s S	Insert string S between the line number and the text. (Default=Tab)

head   **stdin**   **stdout**   **- file**   **-- opt**   **--help**   **--version**

head [*options*] [*files*]

The head command prints the first 10 lines of a file, which is great for previewing the contents:

→ **head myfile**
→ **head myfile* | less**   *Previewing multiple files*

It's also good for previewing the first few lines of output from a pipeline—say, the most recently modified 10 files in the current directory:

→ **ls -lta | head**

Useful options

-n *N*   Print the first *N* lines instead of 10.

-*N*   Same as -n *N*.

-c *N*   Print the first *N* bytes of the file.

-q   Quiet mode: when processing more than one file, don't print a banner above each file. Normally, head prints a banner containing the filename.

---

tail   **stdin**   **stdout**   **- file**   **-- opt**   **--help**   **--version**

tail [*options*] [*files*]

The tail command prints the last 10 lines of a file, and does other tricks as well:

→ **tail myfile**
→ **nl myfile | tail**   *See line numbers too*

The ultra-useful -f option causes tail to watch a file actively while another program is writing to it, displaying new lines as

---

they are written. This is invaluable for watching a Linux log file in active use, as other programs write to it:

```
→ tail -f /var/log/syslog
```

Useful options

-n *N*   Print the last *N* lines of the file instead of 10.

-*N*   Same as -n *N*.

-n +*N*   Print all lines except the first *N*.

-c *N*   Print the last *N* bytes of the file.

-f   Keep the file open, and whenever lines are appended to the file, print them. This is extremely useful. Add the --retry option if the file doesn't exist yet, but you want to wait for it to exist.

-q   Quiet mode: when processing more than one file, don't print a banner above each file. Normally tail prints a banner containing the filename.

---

strings   stdin stdout -file --opt --help --version

```
strings [options] [files]
```

Binary files, such as executable programs and object files, usually contain some readable text. The strings program extracts that text and displays it on standard output. You can discover version information, authors' names, and other useful tidbits with strings:

```
→ strings /usr/bin/who
David MacKenzie
Copyright %s %d Free Software Foundation, Inc.
Report %s bugs to %s
...
```

Combine strings and grep to make your exploring more efficient. Here we look for email addresses:

```
→ strings -n 10 /usr/bin/who | grep '@'
bug-coreutils@gnu.org
```

Useful options

-n *length*   Display only strings with length greater than *length* (the default is 4).

---

od   stdin   stdout   - file   -- opt   --help   --version

od [*options*] [*files*]

When you want to view a binary file, consider od (octal dump) for the job. It copies one or more files to standard output, displaying their data in ASCII, octal, decimal, hexadecimal, or floating point, in various sizes (byte, short, long). For example, this command:

```
→ od -w8 /usr/bin/who
0000000 042577 043114 000401 000001
0000010 000000 000000 000000 000000
0000020 000002 000003 000001 000000
...
```

displays the bytes in binary file */usr/bin/who* in octal, eight bytes per line. The column on the left contains the file offset of each row, again in octal.

If your binary file also contains text, consider the -tc option, which displays character data. For example, binary executables like who contain the string "ELF" at the beginning:

```
→ od -tc -w8 /usr/bin/who | head -3
0000000 177   E   L   F 001 001 001  \0
0000010  \0  \0  \0  \0  \0  \0  \0  \0
0000020 002  \0 003  \0 001  \0  \0  \0
```

Useful options

-N *B*	Display only the first *B* bytes of each file, specified in decimal, hexadecimal (by prepending 0x or 0X), 512-byte blocks (by appending b), kilobytes (by appending k), or megabytes (by appending m). (Default displays the entire file.)
-j *B*	Begin the output at byte *B*+1 of each file; acceptable formats are the same as for the -N option. (Default=0)
-w [*B*]	Display *B* bytes per line; acceptable formats are the same as in the -N option. Using -w by itself is equivalent to -w32. (Default=16)
-s [*B*]	Group each row of bytes into sequences of *B* bytes, separated by whitespace; acceptable formats are the same as in the -N option. Using -s by itself is equivalent to -s3. (Default=2)
-A (d|o|x|n)	Display file offsets in the leftmost column, in decimal (d), octal (o), hexadecimal (x), or not at all (n). (Default=o)
-t(a|c)[z]	Display output in a character format, with nonalphanumeric characters printed as escape sequences (c) or by name (a).
-t(d|o|u|x)[z]	Display output in an integer format, including octal (o), signed decimal (d), unsigned decimal (u), hexadecimal (x).

Appending z to the -t option prints a new column on the righthand side of the output, displaying the printable characters on each line.

File Creation and Editing

Command	Meaning
nano	A simple text editor included by default in popular Linux distros.
emacs	Text editor from Free Software Foundation.

Command	Meaning
vim	Text editor, extension of Unix vi.

To get far with Linux, you must become proficient with one of its text editors. The three major ones are nano, emacs from the Free Software Foundation, and vim, a successor to the Unix editor vi. Teaching these editors fully is beyond the scope of this book, but all have online tutorials, and we list common operations in Table 1. To edit a file, run any of these commands:

→ `nano myfile`
→ `emacs myfile`
→ `vim myfile`

If *myfile* doesn't exist, it is created automatically.

If you share files with Microsoft Windows systems, Linux also has fine programs for editing Microsoft Office documents: LibreOffice (all documents), abiword (Word only), and gnumeric (Excel only). These are probably included in your distro, or you can find them easily through web search.

Creating a File Quickly

You can quickly create an empty file (for later editing) using the touch command:

→ `touch newfile`

or the echo -n command (see "File Properties" on page 69):[10]

→ `echo -n > newfile2`

or write data into a new file by redirecting the output of a program (see "Input/output redirection" on page 33):

→ `echo anything at all > newfile3`

---

10 The -n option prevents a newline character from being written to the file, making it truly empty.

Your Default Editor

Various Linux programs will run an editor when necessary, and usually the default editor is nano or vim. For example, your email program may invoke an editor to compose a new message, and less invokes an editor if you type "v". But what if you want a different default editor? Set the environment variables VISUAL and EDITOR to your choice, for example:

→ **EDITOR=emacs**
→ **VISUAL=emacs**
→ **export EDITOR VISUAL**

Both variables are necessary because different programs check one variable or the other. Set EDITOR and VISUAL in your *~/.bash_profile* startup file if you want your choices made permanent. Any program can be made your default editor as long as it accepts a filename as an argument.

Regardless of how you set these variables, all users should know at least basic commands for each editor in case another program suddenly runs an editor on a critical file.

---

nano　　　　　stdin　　stdout　　- file　　-- opt　　--help　　--version

nano [*options*] [*files*]

Nano is a text editor with basic features. It's included by default in many Linux distros, whereas more powerful editors like emacs and vim might not be. To invoke nano, type

→ **nano**

Nano commands generally involve holding down the control key and typing a letter, such as ^o to save and ^x to quit. Nano helpfully displays common commands at the bottom of its edit window, though some of the vocabulary is a little obscure. (For example, nano uses the term "WriteOut" to mean "save file.") Other commands involve the *meta* key, which is usually the

Escape key or the Alt key. Nano's own documentation notates the meta key as M- (as in M-F to mean "use the meta key and type F"), so we will too. For basic keystrokes, see Table 1. For more documentation, visit *http://nano-editor.org*.

---

emacs   stdin   stdout   **- file**   **-- opt**   **--help**   **--version**

emacs [*options*] [*files*]

emacs is an extremely powerful editing environment with thousands of commands, plus a complete programming language to define your own editing features. To invoke emacs in a new X window, run:

→ **emacs**

To run in a existing shell window:

→ **emacs -nw**

Now to invoke the built-in emacs tutorial, type ^h t.

Most emacs keystroke commands involve the control key (like ^F) or the *meta* key, which is usually the Escape key or the Alt key. emacs's own documentation notates the meta key as M- (as in M-F to mean "use the meta key and type F"), so we will too. For basic keystrokes, see Table 1.

---

vim   stdin   stdout   **- file**   **-- opt**   **--help**   **--version**

vim [*options*] [*files*]

vim is an enhanced version of the old standard Unix editor vi. To invoke the editor in a new X window, run:

→ **gvim**

To run in a existing shell window:

→ `vim`

To run the vim tutorial, run:

→ `vimtutor`

vim is a mode-based editor. It operates usually in two modes, *insert* and *command*, and you must switch between them while editing. Insert mode is for entering text in the usual manner, while command mode is for deleting text, copy/paste, and other operations. For basic keystrokes in normal mode, see Table 1.

Table 1. Basic keystrokes in text editors

Task	emacs	nano	vim
Type text	Just type	Just type	Switch to insert mode if necessary, by typing `i`, then type any text
Save and quit	`^x^s` then `^x^c`	`^o` then `^x`	`:wq`
Quit without saving	`^x^c` Respond "no" when asked to save buffers	`^x` Respond "no" when asked to save	`:q!`
Save	`^x^s`	`^o`	`:w`
Save As	`^x^w`	`^o`, then type a filename	`:w filename`
Undo	`^/` or `^x u`	`M-u`	`u`
Suspend editor (not in X)	`^z`	`^z`	`^z`
Switch to insert mode	*(N/A)*	*(N/A)*	`i`
Switch to command mode	*(N/A)*	*(N/A)*	`ESC`

Task	emacs	nano	vim
Switch to command-line mode	M-x	(N/A)	:
Abort command in progress	^g	^c	ESC
Move forward	^f or right arrow	^f or right arrow	l or right arrow
Move backward	^b or left arrow	^b or left arrow	h or left arrow
Move up	^p or up arrow	^p or up arrow	k or up arrow
Move down	^n or down arrow	^n or down arrow	j or down arrow
Move to next word	M-f	^SPACEBAR	w
Move to previous word	M-b	M-SPACEBAR	b
Move to beginning of line	^a	^a	0
Move to end of line	^e	^e	$
Move down one screen	^v	^v	^f
Move up one screen	M-v	^y	^b
Move to beginning of document	M-<	M-\	gg
Move to end of document	M->	M-/	G
Delete next character	^d	^d	x
Delete previous character	BACKSPACE	BACKSPACE	X
Delete next word	M-d	(N/A)	de
Delete previous word	M-BACKSPACE	(N/A)	db
Delete current line	^a^k	^k	dd
Delete to end of line	^k	. . .	D

Task	emacs	nano	vim
Define region (type this keystroke to mark the beginning of the region, then move the cursor to the end of the desired region)	^SPACEBAR	^^ (control caret)	v
Cut region	^w	^k	d
Copy region	M-w	M-^	y
Paste region	^y	^u	p
Get help	^h	^g	:help
View the manual	^h i	^g	:help

File Properties

stat	Display attributes of files and directories.
wc	Count bytes, words, and lines in a file.
du	Measure disk usage of files and directories.
file	Identify (guess) the type of a file.
touch	Change timestamps of files and directories.
chown	Change owner of files and directories.
chgrp	Change group ownership of files and directories.
chmod	Change protection mode of files and directories.
umask	Set a default mode for new files and directories.
chattr	Change extended attributes of files and directories.
lsattr	List extended attributes of files and directories.

When examining a Linux file, keep in mind that the contents are only half the story. Every file and directory also has attributes that describe its owner, size, access permissions, and other information. The ls -l command (see "Basic File Operations" on page 47) displays some of these attributes, but other commands provide additional information.

---

stat   stdin **stdout** - file **-- opt** **--help** **--version**

stat [*options*] *files*

The stat command lists important attributes of files (by default) or filesystems (-f option). File information looks like:

```
→ stat myfile
  File: 'myfile'
  Size: 1168              Blocks: 8
  IO Block: 4096   regular file
Device: 811h/2065d       Inode: 37224455    Links: 1
Access: (0644/-rw-r--r--)  Uid: ( 600/lisa)
  Gid: ( 620/users)
Access: 2015-11-07 11:15:14.766013415 -0500
Modify: 2015-11-07 11:15:14.722012802 -0500
Change: 2015-11-07 11:15:14.722012802 -0500
 Birth: -
```

and includes the filename, size in bytes (1168), size in blocks (8), file type (Regular File), permissions in octal (0644), permissions in the format of "ls -l" (-rw-r--r--), owner's user ID (600), owner's name (lisa), owner's group ID (620), owner's group name (users), device type (811 in hexadecimal, 2065 in decimal), inode number (37224455), number of hard links (1), and timestamps of the file's most recent access, modification, and status change. Filesystem information looks like:

```
→ stat -f myfile
  File: "myfile"
    ID: f02ed2bb86590cc6 Namelen: 255
Type: ext2/ext3
Block size: 4096         Fundamental block size: 4096
Blocks: Total: 185788077  Free: 108262724
  Available: 98819461
Inodes: Total: 47202304   Free: 46442864
```

and includes the filename (*myfile*), filesystem ID (f02ed2bb86590cc6), maximum allowable length of a filename for that filesystem (255 bytes), filesystem type (ext), block size for the filesystem (4096), the counts of total, free, and available blocks in the filesystem (185788077, 108262724, and 98819461, respectively), and the counts of total and free inodes (47202304 and 46442864, respectively).

The -t option presents the same data but on a single line, without headings. This is handy for processing by shell scripts or other programs:

```
→ stat -t myfile
myfile 1168 8 81a4 600 620 811 37224455 1 0 0
  1446912914 1446912914 1446912914 0 4096
→ stat -tf myfile
myfile f02ed2bb86590cc6 255 ef53 4096 4096
  185788077 108262715 98819452 47202304 46442864
```

Useful options

- -L   Follow symbolic links and report on the file they point to.

- -f   Report on the filesystem containing the file, not the file itself.

- -t   Terse mode: print information on a single line.

---

wc   stdin   stdout   - file   -- opt   --help   --version

wc [*options*] [*files*]

The wc (word count) program prints a count of bytes, words, and lines in (presumably) a text file:

```
→ wc myfile
  18   211 1168 myfile
```

This file has 18 lines, 211 whitespace-delimited words, and 1168 bytes.

Useful options

- -l Print the line count only.

- -w Print the word count only.

- -c Print the byte count only.

- -L Locate the longest line in each file and print its length in bytes.

---

du   stdin   **stdout**   - file   -- opt   --help   --version

du [*options*] [*files|* *directories*]

The du (disk usage) command measures the disk space occupied by files or directories. By default, it measures the current directory and all its subdirectories, printing totals in blocks for each, with a grand total at the bottom:

```
→ du
36    ./Mail
340   ./Files/mine
40    ./Files/bob
416   ./Files
216   ./PC
2404  .
```

It can also measure the size of files:

```
→ du myfile emptyfile hugefile
4       myfile
0       emptyfile
18144   hugefile
```

Useful options

- -b Measure usage in bytes.

- -k Measure usage in kilobytes.

- -m Measure usage in megabytes.

-B *N*	Display sizes in blocks that you define, where 1 block = *N* bytes. (Default = 1024)
-h -H	Print in human-readable units. For example, if two directories are of size 1 gigabyte or 25 kilobytes, respectively, du -h prints 1G and 25K. The -h option uses powers of 1024, whereas -H uses powers of 1000.
-c	Print a total in the last line. This is the default behavior when measuring a directory, but for measuring individual files, provide -c if you want a total.
-L	Follow symbolic links and measure the files they point to.
-s	Print only the total size.

---

file

stdin   stdout   - file   -- opt   --help   --version

```
file [options] files
```

The file command reports the type of a file. The output is an educated guess based on the file content and other factors:

```
→ file /etc/hosts /usr/bin/who letter.docx
/etc/hosts:    ASCII text
/usr/bin/who:  ELF 64-bit LSB executable ...
letter.docx:   Microsoft Word 2007+
```

Useful options

-b	Omit filenames (left column of output).
-i	Print MIME types for the file, such as "text/plain" or "audio/mpeg", instead of the usual output.
-f *name_file*	Read filenames, one per line, from the given *name_file*, and report their types. Afterward, process filenames on the command line as usual.
-L	Follow symbolic links, reporting the type of the destination file instead of the link.

-z	If a file is compressed (see "File Compression and Packaging" on page 110), examine the uncompressed contents to decide the file type, instead of reporting "compressed data."

---

touch

stdin   stdout   - file   **-- opt**   **--help**   **--version**

touch [*options*] *files*

The touch command changes two timestamps associated with a file: its modification time (when the file's data was last changed) and its access time (when the file was last read). To set both timestamps to right now, run:

→ **touch myfile**

You can set these timestamps to arbitrary values, for example:

→ **touch -d "November 18 1975" myfile**

If a given file doesn't exist, touch creates it, offering a handy way to create empty files.

Useful options

-a	Change the access time only.
-m	Change the modification time only.
-c	If the file doesn't exist, don't create it (normally, touch creates it).
-d *timestamp*	Set the file's timestamp(s). A tremendous number of timestamp formats are acceptable, from "12/28/2001 3pm" to "28-May" (the current year is assumed, and a time of midnight) to "next tuesday 13:59" to "0" (midnight today). Experiment and check your work with stat. Full documentation is available from info touch.

-t *timestamp* A more explicit way to set the file's *timestamp*, using the format [[*CC*]*YY*]*MMDDhhmm*[.*ss*], where *CC* is the two-digit century, *YY* is the two-digit year, *MM* is the two-digit month, *DD* is the two-digit day, *hh* is the two-digit hour, *mm* is the two-digit minute, and *ss* is the two-digit second. For example, -t 20030812150047 represents August 12, 2003, at 15:00:47.

---

chown   stdin stdout - file -- opt --help --version

chown [*options*] *user_spec files*

The chown (change owner) command sets the ownership of files and directories. To make user "smith" the owner of several files and a directory, run:

→ **sudo chown smith myfile myfile2 mydir**

The *user_spec* parameter may be any of these possibilities:

- An existing username (or any numeric user ID), to set the owner: chown smith myfile

- An existing username (or any numeric user ID), optionally followed by a colon and an existing group name (or any numeric group ID), to set the owner and group: chown smith:users myfile

- An existing username (or any numeric user ID) followed by a colon, to set the owner *and* to set the group to the invoking user's login group: chown smith: myfile

- An existing group name (or any numeric group ID) preceded by a colon, to set the group only: chown :users myfile

- --reference=*file* to set the same owner and group as another given file

Useful options

`--dereference`	Follow symbolic links and operate on the files they point to.
`-R`	Recursively change permissions within a directory hierarchy.

---

chgrp

`chgrp [options] group_spec files`

The chgrp (change group) command sets the group ownership of files and directories:

→ `chgrp smith myfile myfile2 mydir`

The *group_spec* parameter may be any of these possibilities:

- A group name or numeric group ID
- `--reference=file`, to set the same group ownership as another given file

See "Group Management" on page 172 for more information on groups.

Useful options

`--dereference`	Follow symbolic links and operate on the files they point to.
`-R`	Recursively change the ownership within a directory hierarchy.

chmod [*options*] *permissions files*

The chmod (change mode) command protects files and directories from unauthorized users on the same system, by setting access permissions. Typical permissions are read, write, and execute, and they may be limited to the file owner, the file's group owner, and/or other users. The permissions argument can take three different forms:

- --reference=*file*, to set the same permissions as another given file.

- An octal number, up to four digits long, that specifies the file's *absolute* permissions in bits, as in Figure 6. The leftmost digit is special (described later) and the second, third, and fourth represent the file's owner, the file's group, and all users, respectively.

- One or more strings specifying *absolute or relative* permissions (i.e., relative to the file's existing permissions). For example, a+r makes a file readable by all users.

The most common permissions are:

→ **chmod 600 myfile**	*Private file for you*
→ **chmod 644 myfile**	*Everyone can read; you can write*
→ **chmod 700 mydir**	*Private directory for you*
→ **chmod 755 mydir**	*Everyone can read; you can write*

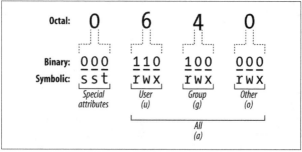

Figure 6. File permission bits explained

In the third form, each string consists of three parts:

Scope (optional)
> u for user, g for group, o for other users not in the group, a for all users. The default is a.

Command
> + to add permissions; - to remove permissions; or = to set absolute permissions, ignoring existing ones.

Permissions
> r for read, w for write/modify, x for execute (for directories, this is permission to cd into the directory), X for conditional execute (explained later), u to duplicate the user permissions, g to duplicate the group permissions, o to duplicate the "other users" permissions, s for setuid or setgid, and t for the sticky bit.

For example, ug+rw would add read and write permission for the user and the group, a-x (or just -x) would remove execute permission for everyone, and o=r would directly set the "other users" permissions to read only. You can combine these strings by separating them with commas, such as ug+rw,a-x.

Conditional execute permission (X) means the same as x, except that it succeeds only if the file is already executable, or if the file is a directory. Otherwise, it has no effect.

Setuid and setgid, when applied to executable files (programs and scripts), have a powerful effect. Suppose we have an executable file *F* owned by user "smith" and the group "friends". If file *F* has setuid (set user ID) enabled, then anyone who runs *F* will "become" user "smith," with all her rights and privileges, for the duration of the program. Likewise, if *F* has setgid (set group ID) enabled, anyone who executes *F* becomes a member of the "friends" group for the duration of the program. As you might imagine, setuid and setgid can impact system security, so don't use them unless you *really* know what you're doing. One misplaced chmod +s can leave your whole system vulnerable to attack.

The sticky bit, most commonly used for */tmp* directories, controls removal of files in that directory. Normally, if you have write permission in a directory, you can delete or move files within it, even if you don't have this access to the files themselves. Inside a directory with the sticky bit set, you need write permission on a file in order to delete or move it.

Useful options

-R   Recursively change the ownership within a directory hierarchy.

---

umask   stdin   **stdout**   - file   -- opt   --help   --version

umask [*options*] [*mask*]

The umask command sets or displays your default mode for creating files and directories—whether they are readable, writable, and/or executable by yourself, your group, and the world:

```
→ umask
0002
→ umask -S
u=rwx,g=rwx,o=rx
```

Let's start with some technical talk and follow with common-sense advice. A umask is a binary (base two) value, though it is commonly presented in octal (base eight). It defines your default protection mode by combining with the octal value 0666 for files and 0777 for directories, using the binary operation NOT AND. For example, the umask 0002 yields a default file mode of 0664:

```
0666 NOT AND 0002
= 000110110110 NOT AND 000000000010
= 000110110110 AND 111111111101
= 000110110100
= 0664
```

Similarly for directories, 0002 NOT AND 0777 yields a default mode of 0775.

If that explanation seems from outer space, here are some simple recipes. Use mask 0022 to give yourself full privileges, and all others read/execute privileges only:

```
→ umask 0022
→ touch newfile && mkdir dir
→ ls -ldG newfile dir
-rw-r--r--  1 smith      0 Nov 11 12:25 newfile
drwxr-xr-x  2 smith   4096 Nov 11 12:25 dir
```

Use mask 0002 to give yourself and your default group full privileges, and read/execute to others:

```
→ umask 0002
→ touch newfile && mkdir dir
→ ls -ldG newfile dir
-rw-rw-r--  1 smith      0 Nov 11 12:26 newfile
drwxrwxr-x  2 smith   4096 Nov 11 12:26 dir
```

Use mask 0077 to give yourself full privileges with nothing for anyone else:

```
→ umask 0077
→ touch newfile && mkdir dir
→ ls -ldG newfile dir
```

```
-rw-------   1 smith       0 Nov 11 12:27 newfile
drwx------   2 smith    4096 Nov 11 12:27 dir
```

---

chattr   stdin   stdout   - file   -- opt   --help   --version

chattr [*options*] [+ - =]*attributes* [*files*]

If you grew up with other Unix systems, you might be surprised that Linux files can have additional attributes beyond their access permissions. If a file is on an "ext" filesystem (ext2, ext3, etc.), you can set these extended attributes with the chattr (change attribute) command and list them with lsattr.

As with chmod, attributes may be added (+) or removed (-) relatively, or set absolutely (=). For example, to keep a file compressed and nondumpable, run:

→ **chattr +cd myfile**

Attribute	Meaning
a	Append-only: appends are permitted to this file, but it cannot otherwise be edited. Root only.
A	Accesses not timestamped: accesses to this file don't update its access timestamp (atime).
c	Compressed: data is transparently compressed on writes and uncompressed on reads.
d	Don't dump: tell the dump program to ignore this file when making backups (see "Backups and Remote Storage" on page 137).
i	Immutable: file cannot be changed or deleted (root only).
j	Journaled data (ext3 filesystems only).
s	Secure deletion: if deleted, this file's data is overwritten with zeros.
S	Synchronous update: changes are written to disk immediately.
u	Undeletable: file cannot be deleted.

There are a few other attributes too, some of them obscure or experimental. See the manpage for details.

Useful options

-R Recursively process directories.

---

lsattr   stdin   **stdout**   - file   **-- opt**   **--help**   --version

lsattr [options] [files]

If you set extended attributes with chattr, you can view them with lsattr (list attributes). The output uses the same letters as chattr; for example, this file is immutable and undeletable:

→ **lsattr myfile**
-u--i--- myfile

With no files specified, lsattr prints the attributes of all files in the current directory.

Useful options

-R Recursively process directories.

-a List all files, including those whose names begin with a dot.

-d If listing a directory, do not list its contents, just the directory itself.

File Location

find   Locate files in a directory hierarchy.

xargs   Process a list of located files (and much more).

locate   Create an index of files, and search the index for string.

which   Locate executables in your search path (command).

type   Locate executables in your search path (bash built-in).

---

whereis   Locate executables, documentation, and source files.

Linux systems can contain hundreds of thousands of files easily. How can you find a particular file when you need to? The first step is to organize your files logically into directories in some thoughtful manner, but there are several other ways to find files, depending on what you're looking for.

For finding any file, find is a brute-force program that slogs file by file through a directory hierarchy to locate a target. locate is much faster, searching through a prebuilt index that you generate as needed. (Some distros generate the index nightly by default.)

For finding programs, the which and type commands check all directories in your shell search path. type is built into the bash shell (and therefore available only when you're running bash), while which is a program (normally */usr/bin/which*); type is faster and can detect shell aliases.[11] In contrast, whereis examines a known set of directories, rather than your search path.

---

find   stdin   **stdout**   - file   -- opt   **--help**   **--version**

find [*directories*] [*expression*]

The find command searches one or more directories (and their subdirectories recursively) for files matching certain criteria. It is very powerful, with over 50 options, and unfortunately, a rather unusual syntax. Here are some simple examples that search the entire filesystem from the current directory (indicated by a dot):

Find a particular file named *myfile*:

---

11 The tcsh shell performs some trickery to make which detect aliases.

```
→ find . -type f -name myfile -print
./myfile
```

Print filenames beginning with "myfile" (notice how the wild-card is escaped so the shell ignores it):

```
→ find . -type f -name myfile\* -print
./myfile.zip
./myfile3
./myfile
./myfile2
```

Print all directory names:

```
→ find . -type d -print
.
./jpegexample
./dir2
./mydir
./mydir/dir
./dir1
./dir3
./d
```

Useful options

-name *pattern* -path *pattern* -lname *pattern*	The name (-name), pathname (-path), or symbolic link target (-lname) of the desired file must match this shell pattern, which may include shell wildcards *, ?, and []. (You must escape the wildcards, however, so they are ignored by the shell and passed literally to find.) Paths are relative to the directory tree being searched.
-iname *pattern* -ipath *pattern* -ilname *pattern*	The -iname, -ipath, and -ilname options are the same as -name, -path, and -lname, respectively, but are case-insensitive.
-regex *regexp*	The path (relative to the directory tree being searched) must match the given regular expression.

`-type t`	Locate only files of type *t*. This includes plain files (f), directories (d), symbolic links (l), block devices (b), character devices (c), named pipes (p), and sockets (s).
`-atime N` `-ctime N` `-mtime N`	File was last accessed (`-atime`), last modified (`-mtime`), or had a status change (`-ctime`) exactly *N* *24 hours ago. Use +*N* for "greater than *N*," or -*N* for "less than *N*."
`-amin N` `-cmin N` `-mmin N`	File was last accessed (`-amin`), last modified (`-mmin`), or had a status change (`-cmin`) exactly *N* minutes ago. Use +*N* for "greater than *N*," or -*N* for "less than *N*."
`-anewer other_file` `-cnewer other_file` `-newer other_file`	File was accessed (`-anewer`), modified (`-newer`), or had a status change (`-cnewer`) more recently than *other_file*.
`-maxdepth N` `-mindepth N`	Consider files at least (`-mindepth`) or at most (`-maxdepth`) *N* levels deep in the directory tree being searched.
`-follow`	Dereference symbolic links.
`-depth`	Proceed using depth-first search: completely search a directory's contents (recursively) before operating on the directory itself.
`-xdev`	Limit the search to a single filesystem (i.e., don't cross device boundaries).
`-size N[bckw]`	Consider files of size *N*, which can be given in blocks (b), one-byte characters (c), kilobytes (k), or two-byte words (w). Use +*N* for "greater than *N*," or -*N* for "less than *N*."
`-empty`	File has zero size, and is a regular file or directory.
`-user name`	File is owned by the given user.
`-group name`	File is owned by the given group.

| -perm *mode* | File has permissions equal to mode. Use - *mode* to check that *all* of the given bits are set, or +*mode* to check that *any* of the given bits are set. |

You can group and negate parts of the expression with the following operators:

expression1 -a *expression2*

> And. (This is the default if two expressions appear side by side, so the "-a" is optional.)

expression1 -o *expression2*

> Or.

! expression
-not expression

> Negate the expression.

(expression)

> Precedence markers, just like in algebra class. Evaluate what's in parentheses first. You may need to escape these from the shell with "\".

expression1 , expression2

> Same as the comma operator in the C programming language. Evaluate both expressions and return the value of the second one.

Once you've specified the search criteria, you can tell find to perform these actions on files that match the criteria.

Useful options

| -print | Simply print the path to the file, relative to the search directory. |
| -printf *string* | Print the given string, which may have substitutions applied to it in the manner of the C library function, printf(). See the manpage for the full list of outputs. |

-print0	Like -print, but instead of separating each line of output with a newline character, use a null (ASCII 0) character. Use when piping the output of find to another program, and your list of filenames may contain space characters. Of course, the receiving program must be capable of reading and parsing these null-separated lines (e.g., xargs -0).
-exec *cmd* ;	Invoke the given shell command, *cmd*. Make sure to escape any shell metacharacters, including the required, final semicolon, so they are not immediately evaluated on the command line. Also, the symbol "{}" (make sure to quote or escape it) represents the path to the file found. A full example is: `find . -exec ls '{}' \;`
-ok *cmd* ;	Same as -exec, but also prompts the user before invoking each command.
-ls	Perform the command ls -dils on the file.

---

xargs

stdin   stdout   - file   -- opt   **--help**   **--version**

xargs [*options*] [*command*]

xargs is one of the oddest yet most powerful commands available to the shell. It reads lines of text from standard input, turns them into commands, and executes them. This might not sound exciting, but xargs has some unique uses, particularly for processing a list of files you've located. Suppose you made a file named *important* that lists important files, one per line:

```
→ cat important
/home/jsmith/mail/love-letters
/usr/local/lib/critical_stuff
/etc/passwd
...
```

With xargs, you can process each of these files easily with other Linux commands. For instance, the following command runs the ls -l command on all the listed files:

```
→ cat important | xargs ls -l
```

Similarly, you can view the files with less:

```
→ cat important | xargs less
```

and even delete them with rm:

```
→ cat important | xargs rm -f        Careful! Destructive!
```

Each of these pipelines reads the list of files from *important* and produces and runs new Linux commands based on the list. The power begins when the input list doesn't come from a file, but from another command writing to standard output. In particular, the find command, which prints a list of files on standard output, makes a great partner for xargs. For example, to search your current directory hierarchy for files containing the word "tomato":

```
→ find . -type f -print | xargs grep -l tomato
./findfile1
./findfile2
→ cat findfile1
This file contains the word tomato.
```

This power comes with one warning: if any of the files located by find contains whitespace in its name, this will confuse grep. If one file is named (say) *my stuff*, then the grep command constructed is:

```
grep -l tomato my stuff
```

which tells grep to process *two* files named *my* and *stuff*. Oops! Now imagine if the program had been rm instead of grep. You'd be telling rm to delete the wrong files! To avoid this problem, always use find -print0 instead of -print, which separates lines with ASCII null characters instead of newline characters, combined with xargs -0, which expects ASCII nulls:

```
→ find . -type f -print0 | xargs -0 grep -l tomato
```

We have barely scratched the surface of the xargs command, so continue experimenting! (With harmless commands like grep and ls at first!)

Useful options

- `-n k`   Feed *k* lines of input to each executed command. The common `-n1` guarantees that each execution will process only one line of input. Otherwise, xargs may pass multiple lines of input to a single command.

- `-0`   Set the end-of-line character for input to be ASCII zero rather than whitespace, and treat all characters literally. Use this when the input is coming from find `-print0`.

---

xargs Versus Backquotes

If you remember "Quoting" on page 36, you might realize that some xargs tricks can be accomplished with backquotes:

```
→ cat file_list | xargs rm -f        With xargs
→ rm -f `cat file_list`              With backquotes
→ rm -f $(cat file_list)             With $()
```

While these commands do similar things, the last two can fail if the command line gets so long, after the output of cat is expanded, that it exceeds the maximum length of a shell command line. xargs writes to standard output, rather than appending to the command line, so it's safer and more suitable for large or risky operations.

```
locate [options]
```

The locate command, with its partner updatedb, creates an index (database) of file locations that is quickly searchable.[12] If you plan to search for many files over time in a directory hierarchy that doesn't change much, locate is a good choice. For locating a single file or performing more complex processing of found files, use find.

Some distros automatically index the entire filesystem on a regular basis (e.g., once a day), so you can simply run locate and it will work. But if you ever need to create an index yourself of a directory and all its subdirectories (say, storing it in */tmp/ myindex*), run:

→ **updatedb -l0 -U** *directory* **-o /tmp/myindex**

(Note that -l0 is a lowercase L followed by a zero, not the number 10.) Then to search for a string in the index:

→ **locate -d /tmp/myindex** *string*

locate has an interesting, optional security feature. You can create an index that, when searched, will display only files that the user is permitted to see. So if the superuser created an index of a protected directory, a nonsuperuser could search it but not see the protected files. This is done by omitting the -l0 option to updatedb and running it as root:

→ **sudo updatedb -U** *directory* **-o /tmp/myindex**

---

12 Our locate command comes from a package called "mlocate." Some systems have an older package called "slocate" with slightly different usage. If you have slocate, simply type slocate instead of updatedb in our examples.

Indexing options for updatedb

-u	Create index from the root directory downward.
-U *directory*	Create index from *directory* downward.
-l (0|1)	Turn security off (0) or on (1). The default is 1.
-e *directories*	Exclude one or more directories from the index. Separate their paths by commas.
-o *outfile*	Write the index to file *outfile*.

Search options for locate

-d *index*	Indicate which index to use (in our example, */tmp/myindex*).
-i	Case-insensitive search.
-r *regexp*	Search for files matching the given regular expression.

---

which   stdin   **stdout**   - file   -- opt   **--help**   **--version**

which *file*

The which command locates an executable file in your shell's search path. If you've been invoking a program by typing its name:

→ **who**

the which command tells you where this command is located:

→ **which who**
/usr/bin/who

You can even find the which program itself:

→ **which which**
/usr/bin/which

If several programs in your search path have the same name (e.g., */usr/bin/who* and */usr/local/bin/who*), which reports only the first.

---

type

```
type [options] commands
```

The type command, like which, locates an executable file in your shell's search path:

```
→ type grep who
grep is /bin/grep
who is /usr/bin/who
```

However, type is built into the bash shell, whereas which is a program on disk:

```
→ type which type rm if
which is /usr/bin/which
type is a shell builtin
rm is aliased to `/bin/rm -i'
if is a shell keyword
```

As a built-in shell command, type is faster than which; however, it's available only in certain shells such as bash.

---

whereis

```
whereis [options] files
```

The whereis command attempts to locate the given files by searching a hardcoded list of directories. It can find executables, documentation, and source code. whereis is somewhat quirky because its list of directories might not include the ones you need.

```
→ whereis vim
vim: /usr/bin/vim /etc/vim /usr/share/vim …
```

Useful options

-b	List only executables (-b), manpages (-m), or source code
-m	files (-s).
-s	

-B *dirs*... -f	Search for executables (-B), manpages (-M), or source code
-M *dirs*... -f	files (-S) only in the given directories. You must follow the
-S *dirs*... -f	directory list with the -f option before listing the files you
	seek.

File Text Manipulation

grep	Find lines in a file that match a regular expression.
cut	Extract columns from a file.
paste	Append columns.
tr	Translate characters into other characters.
expand, unexpand	Convert between tabs and spaces.
sort	Sort lines of text by various criteria.
uniq	Locate identical lines in a file.
tee	Copy a file *and* print it on standard output, simultaneously.

Perhaps Linux's greatest strength is text manipulation: massaging a text file (or standard input) into a desired form by applying transformations, often in a pipeline. Any program that reads standard input and writes standard output falls into this category, but here we'll present some of the most important tools.

grep

```
grep [options] pattern [files]
```

The grep command is one of the most consistently useful and powerful in the Linux arsenal. Its premise is simple: given one or more files, print all lines in those files that match a particular regular expression pattern. For example, if a file *randomlines* contains these lines:

```
The quick brown fox jumped over the lazy dogs!
My very eager mother just served us nine pancakes.
Film at eleven.
```

and we search for all lines containing "pancake", we get:

```
→ grep pancake randomlines
My very eager mother just served us nine pancakes.
```

Now we use a regular expression to match lines ending in an exclamation point:

```
→ grep '\!$' randomlines
The quick brown fox jumped over the lazy dogs!
```

grep can use two different types of regular expressions, which it calls *basic* and *extended*. They are equally powerful, just different, and you may prefer one over the other based on your experience with other grep implementations. The basic syntax is in Table 2. Regular expressions are well worth your time to learn. Other powerful Linux programs use them as well, such as sed and perl.

Useful options

-v	Print only lines that *do not* match the regular expression.
-l	Print only the *names* of files that contain matching lines, not the lines themselves.

`-L`	Print only the names of files that *do not* contain matching lines.
`-c`	Print only a count of matching lines.
`-n`	In front of each line of matching output, print its original line number.
`-b`	In front of each line of matching output, print the byte offset of the line in the input file.
`-i`	Case-insensitive match.
`-w`	Match only complete words (i.e., words that match the entire regular expression).
`-x`	Match only complete lines (i.e., lines that match the entire regular expression). Overrides `-w`.
`-A N`	After each matching line, print the next *N* lines from its file.
`-B N`	Before each matching line, print the previous *N* lines from its file.
`-C N`	Same as -A *N* -B *N*: print *N* lines (from the original file) above *and* below each matching line.
`--color=always`	Highlight the matched text in color, for better readability.
`-r`	Recursively search all files in a directory and its subdirectories.
`-E`	Use extended regular expressions. See `egrep`.
`-F`	Use lists of fixed strings instead of regular expressions. See `fgrep`.

egrep

```
egrep [options] pattern [files]
```

The egrep command is just like grep, but uses a different ("extended") language for regular expressions. It's the same as grep -E.

Table 2. Regular expressions for grep and egrep

Regular expression		
Plain	Extended	Meaning
.		Any single character.
[...]		Match any single character in this list.
[^...]		Match any single character NOT in this list.
(...)		Grouping.
|	|	Or.
^		Beginning of a line.
$		End of a line.
\<		Beginning of a word.
\>		End of a word.
[:alnum:]		Any alphanumeric character.
[:alpha:]		Any alphabetic character.
[:cntrl:]		Any control character.
[:digit:]		Any digit.
[:graph:]		Any graphic character.
[:lower:]		Any lowercase letter.
[:print:]		Any printable character.
[:punct:]		Any punctuation mark.
[:space:]		Any whitespace character.

Regular expression		
Plain	Extended	Meaning
[:upper:]		Any uppercase letter.
[:xdigit:]		Any hexadecimal digit.
*		Zero or more repetitions of a regular expression.
\+	+	One or more repetitions of a regular expression.
\?	?	Zero or one occurrence of a regular expression.
\{n\}	{n}	Exactly *n* repetitions of a regular expression.
\{n,\}	{n,}	*n* or more repetitions of a regular expression.
\{n,m\}	{n,m}	Between *n* and *m* (inclusive) repetitions of a regular expression, $n < m$.
\c		The literal character *c*, even if *c* is a special regular expression character. For example, use * to match an asterisk or \\ to match a backslash. Alternatively, put the literal character in square brackets, like [*] or [\].

grep and End-of-Line Characters

When you match the end of a line ($) with grep, text files created on Microsoft Windows or Mac OS X systems may produce odd results. Each operating system has a different standard for ending a line. On Linux, each line in a text file ends with a newline character (ASCII 10). On Windows, text lines end with a carriage return (ASCII 13) followed by a newline character. And on OS X, a text file might end its lines with newlines or carriage returns alone. If grep isn't matching the ends of lines properly, check for non-Linux end-of-line characters with cat -v, which displays carriage returns as ^M:

→ **cat -v dosfile.txt**
Uh-oh! This file seems to end its lines with^M
carriage returns before the newlines.^M

To remove the carriage returns, use the tr -d command:

```
→ tr -d '\r' < dosfile.txt > linuxfile.txt
→ cat -v linuxfile.txt
Uh-oh! This file seems to end its lines with
carriage returns before the newlines.
```

---

fgrep
stdin stdout -file --opt --help --version

```
fgrep [options] [fixed_strings] [files]
```

The fgrep command is just like grep, but instead of accepting a
regular expression, it accepts a list of fixed strings, separated by
newlines. It's the same as grep -F. For example, if you have a
dictionary file full of strings, one per line:

```
→ cat my_dictionary_file
aardvark
aback
abandon
...
```

you can conveniently search for those strings in a set of input
files:

```
→ fgrep -f my_dictionary_file story
a little aardvark who went to
visit the abbot at the abbey.
```

Normally, you'll use the lowercase -f option to make fgrep
read the fixed strings from a file. You can also read the fixed
strings on the command line using quoting, but it's a bit trick-
ier. To search for the strings "one", "two", and "three" in a file,
you'd type:

```
→ fgrep 'one          Note we are typing newline characters
two
three' myfile
```

fgrep is convenient when searching for nonalphanumeric characters like * and { because they are treated literally, not as regular expression characters.

---

cut

```
cut -(b|c|f)range [options] [files]
```

The cut command extracts columns of text from files. A "column" is defined by character offsets (e.g., the nineteenth character of each line):

```
→ cut -c19 myfile
```

or by byte offsets (which are different from characters if your language has multibyte characters):

```
→ cut -b19 myfile
```

or by delimited fields (e.g., the fifth field in each line of a comma-delimited file, *data.csv*):

```
→ cat data.csv
one,two,three,four,five,six,seven
ONE,TWO,THREE,FOUR,FIVE,SIX,SEVEN
1,2,3,4,5,6,7
→ cut -f5 -d, data.csv
five
FIVE
5
```

You aren't limited to printing a single column: you can provide a range (3-16), a comma-separated sequence (3,4,5,6,8,16), or both (3,4,8-16). For ranges, if you omit the first number (-16), a 1 is assumed (1-16); if you omit the last number (5-), the end of line is used.

Useful options

-d C	Use character C as the *input* delimiter character between fields for the -f option. By default it's a tab character.
--output-delimiter=C	Use character C as the *output* delimiter character between fields for -f. By default it's a tab character.
-s	Suppress (don't print) lines that don't contain the delimiter character.

---

paste

stdin   stdout   -file   --opt   --help   --version

```
paste [options] [files]
```

The paste command is the opposite of cut: it treats several files as vertical columns and combines them on standard output:

```
→ cat letters
A
B
C
→ cat numbers
1
2
3
4
5
→ paste numbers letters
1   A
2   B
3   C
4
5
→ paste letters numbers
A   1
B   2
```

```
C   3
    4
    5
```

Useful options

-d *delimiters*	Use the given *delimiters* characters between columns; the default is a tab character. Provide a single character (-d:) to be used always, or a list of characters (-dxyz) to be applied in sequence on each line (the first delimiter is x, then y, then z, then x, then y, ...).
-s	Sideways: transpose the rows and columns of output: → **paste -s letters numbers** A B C 1 2 3 4 5

---

tr   stdin   stdout   - file   -- opt   **--help**   **--version**

tr [*options*] *charset1* [*charset2*]

The tr command performs some simple, useful translations of one set of characters into another. For example, to capitalize everything in a file:

```
→ cat wonderfulfile
This is a very wonderful file.
→ cat wonderfulfile | tr 'a-z' 'A-Z'
THIS IS A VERY WONDERFUL FILE.
```

or to change all vowels into asterisks:

```
→ cat wonderfulfile | tr aeiouAEIOU '*'
Th*s *s * v*ry w*nd*rf*l f*l*.
```

or to delete all vowels:

```
→ cat wonderfulfile | tr -d aeiouAEIOU
Ths s  vry wndrfl fl.
```

As a practical example, delete all carriage returns from a DOS text file so it's more compatible with Linux text utilities like grep:

```
→ tr -d '\r' < dosfile.txt > linuxfile.txt
```

tr translates the first character in *charset1* into the first character in *charset2*, the second into the second, the third into the third, and so on. If the length of *charset1* is *N*, only the first *N* characters in *charset2* are used. (If *charset1* is longer than *charset2*, see the -t option.)

Character sets can have the following forms:

Form	Meaning
ABDG	The sequence of characters A, B, D, G.
A-Z	The range of characters from A to Z.
[x*y]	*y* repetitions of the character *x*.
[:*class*:]	The same character classes ([:alnum:], [:digit:], etc.) accepted by grep.

tr also understands the escape characters "\a" (^G = alert by ringing bell), "\b" (^H = backspace), "\f" (^L = formfeed), "\n" (^J = newline), "\r" (^M = return), "\t" (^I = tab), and "\v" (^K = vertical tab) accepted by printf (see "Screen Output" on page 203), as well as the notation \nnn to mean the character with octal value *nnn*.

tr is great for quick and simple translations, but for more powerful jobs consider sed, awk, or perl.

Useful options

-d   Delete the characters in *charset1* from the input.

-s   Eliminate adjacent duplicates (found in *charset1*) from the input. For example, tr -s aeiouAEIOU would squeeze adjacent, duplicate vowels to be single vowels (reeeeeeally would become really).

- -c   Complement: operate on all characters *not* found in `charset1`.

- -t   If `charset1` is longer than `charset2`, make them the same length by
       truncating `charset1`. If -t is not present, the last character of `charset2`
       is (invisibly) repeated until `charset2` is the same length as `charset1`.

---

expand

stdin   **stdout**   **- file**   **-- opt**   **--help**   **--version**

```
expand [options] [files]
unexpand [options] [files]
```

The expand command converts tab characters to an equivalent-looking number of space characters, and unexpand does the opposite. By default, a tab stop occurs every eight spaces, but you can change this with options. Both programs write to standard output by default.

```
→ expand tabfile > spacefile
→ expand spacefile > tabfile
```

To check whether a file contains spaces or tabs, use the cat -T command, which displays tabs as ^I, or the od -c command, which displays tabs as \t.

Useful options

- -t *N*   Specify that one tab stop occurs every *N* spaces.

sort   stdin   stdout   - file   -- opt   --help   --version

```
sort [options] [files]
```

The sort command prints lines of text in alphabetical order, or
sorted by some other rule you specify. All provided files are
concatenated, and the result is sorted and printed:

```
→ cat threeletters
def
xyz
abc
→ sort threeletters
abc
def
xyz
```

Useful options

- -f   Case-insensitive sorting.

- -n   Sort numerically (i.e., 9 comes before 10) instead of alphabetically (10
           comes before 9 because it begins with a "1").

- -g   Another numerical sorting method with a different algorithm that,
           among other things, recognizes scientific notation (7.4e3 means "7.4
           times ten to the third power," or 7400). Run info sort for full
           technical details.

- -u   Unique sort: ignore duplicate lines. (If used with - c for checking sorted
           files, fail if any consecutive lines are identical.)

- -c   Don't sort, just check if the input is already sorted. If it is, print nothing;
           otherwise, print an error message.

- -b   Ignore leading whitespace in lines.

- -r   Reverse the output: sort from greatest to least.

- -t *X*   Use *X* as the field delimiter for the - k option.

- -k *key* Choose sorting keys. (Combine with - t to choose a separator character
           between keys.)

A sorting key indicates a portion of a line to consider when sorting, instead of the entire line. An example could be the fifth character of each line. Normally, sort would consider these lines to be in sorted order:

```
aaaaz
bbbby
```

but if your sorting key is "the fifth character of each line," denoted -k1.5, then the lines are reversed because y comes before z. A more practical example involves this file of names and addresses:

```
→ cat people
George Washington,123 Main Street,New York
Abraham Lincoln,54 First Avenue,San Francisco
John Adams,39 Tremont Street,Boston
```

An ordinary sort would display the "Abraham Lincoln" line first. But if you consider each line as three comma-separated values, you can sort on the second value with:

```
→ sort -k2 -t, people
George Washington,123 Main Street,New York
John Adams,39 Tremont Street,Boston
Abraham Lincoln,54 First Avenue,San Francisco
```

where "123 Main Street" is first alphabetically. Likewise, you can sort on the city (third value) with:

```
→ sort -k3 -t, people
John Adams,39 Tremont Street,Boston
George Washington,123 Main Street,New York
Abraham Lincoln,54 First Avenue,San Francisco
```

and see that Boston comes up first alphabetically. The general syntax -k F1[.C1][,F2[.C2]] means:

Item	Meaning	Default if not supplied
F1	Starting field	Required
C1	Starting position within field 1	1

Item	Meaning	Default if not supplied
F2	Ending field	Last field
C2	Starting position within ending field	1

So sort -k1.5 sorts based on the first field, beginning at its fifth character; and sort -k2.8,5 means "from the eighth character of the second field, up to the first character of the fifth field." The -t option changes the behavior of -k so it considers delimiter characters such as commas rather than spaces.

You can repeat the -k option to define multiple keys, which will be applied from first to last as found on the command line.

---

uniq   stdin   stdout   - file   -- opt   --help   --version

```
uniq [options] [files]
```

The uniq command operates on consecutive, duplicate lines of text. For example, if you have a file *myfile*:

```
→ cat letters2
a
b
b
c
b
```

then uniq would detect and process (in whatever way you specify) the two consecutive b's, but not the third b:

```
→ uniq letters2
a
b
c
b
```

uniq is often used after sorting a file:

```
→ sort letters2 | uniq
a
b
c
```

In this case, only a single b remains because all three were made adjacent by sort, then collapsed to one by uniq. Also, you can count duplicate lines instead of eliminating them:

```
→ sort letters2 | uniq -c
      1 a
      3 b
      1 c
```

Useful options

- -c   Count adjacent duplicate lines.

- -i   Case-insensitive operation.

- -u   Print unique lines only.

- -d   Print duplicate lines only.

- -s N Skip the first N characters on each line when detecting duplicates.

- -f N Ignore the first N whitespace-separated fields on each line when detecting duplicates.

- -w N Consider only the first N characters on each line when detecting duplicates. If used with -s or -f, sort will ignore the specified number of characters or fields first, then consider the next N characters.

---

tee   stdin   stdout   - file   -- opt   --help   --version

```
tee [options] files
```

Like the cat command, the tee command copies standard input to standard output unaltered. Simultaneously, however, it also copies that same standard input to one or more files. tee is most often found in the middle of pipelines, writing some intermediate data to a file while also passing it to the next command in the pipeline:

```
→ who | tee original_who | sort
barrett    pts/1     Sep 22 21:15
byrnes     pts/0     Sep 15 13:51
silver     :0        Sep 23 20:44
silver     pts/2     Sep 22 21:18
```

This command line produces the sorted output of who on screen, but also writes the original, unsorted output of who to the file *original_who*:

```
→ cat original_who
silver     :0        Sep 23 20:44
byrnes     pts/0     Sep 15 13:51
barrett    pts/1     Sep 22 21:15
silver     pts/2     Sep 22 21:18
```

and then passes along that same output to the rest of the pipeline (sort), producing sorted output on screen.

Useful options

- -a   Append instead of overwriting files.

- -i   Ignore interrupt signals.

More Powerful Manipulations

We've just touched the tip of the iceberg for Linux text filtering. Linux has hundreds of filters that produce ever more complex manipulations of the data. But with great power comes a great learning curve, too much for a short book. Here are a few filters to get you started.

awk

AWK is a pattern-matching language. It matches data by regular expression and then performs actions based on the data. Here are a few simple examples for processing a text file, *myfile*.

Print the second and fourth word on each line:

```
→ awk '{print $2, $4}' myfile
```

Print all lines that are shorter than 60 characters:

```
→ awk 'length < 60 {print}' myfile
```

sed

Like AWK, sed is a pattern-matching engine that can perform manipulations on lines of text. Its syntax is closely related to that of vim and the line editor ed. Here are some trivial examples.

Print the file with all occurrences of the string "me" changed to "YOU":

```
→ sed 's/me/YOU/g' myfile
```

Print the file with the first 10 lines removed:

```
→ sed '1,10d' myfile
```

m4

m4 is a macro-processing language and command. It locates keywords within a file and substitutes values for them. For example, given this file:

```
→ cat substitutions
My name is NAME and I am AGE years old.
ifelse(QUOTE,yes,Learn Linux today!)
```

see what m4 does with substitutions for NAME, AGE, and QUOTE:

```
→ m4 -DNAME=Sandy substitutions
My name is Sandy and I am AGE years old.
```

```
→ m4 -DNAME=Sandy -DAGE=25 substitutions
My name is Sandy and I am 25 years old.

→ m4 -DNAME=Sandy -DAGE=25 -DQUOTE=yes substitutions
My name is Sandy and I am 25 years old.
Learn Linux today!
```

Perl, PHP, Python, Ruby

Perl, PHP, Python, and Ruby are full-fledged programming languages powerful enough to build complete, robust applications. See "Beyond Shell Scripting" on page 255 for references.

File Compression and Packaging

tar	Package multiple files into a single file.
gzip	Compress files with GNU Zip.
gunzip	Uncompress GNU Zip files.
bzip2	Compress files in BZip format.
bunzip2	Uncompress BZip files.
bzcat	Compress/uncompress BZip files via standard input/output.
compress	Compress files with traditional Unix compression.
uncompress	Uncompress files with traditional Unix compression.
zcat	Compress/uncompress file via standard input/output (gzip or compress).
zip	Compress files in Windows Zip format.
unzip	Uncompress Windows Zip files.
munpack	Extract MIME data to files.
mpack	Convert a file into MIME format.

Linux can compress files into a variety of formats and uncompress them. The most popular formats are GNU Zip (gzip), whose compressed files are named with the *.gz* extension, and BZip, which uses the *.bz2* extension. Other common formats include Zip files from Windows systems (.*zip* extension), xz files (.*xz* and .*lzma* extensions), and occasionally, classic Unix compression (.*Z* extension).

A related technology involves converting binary files into textual formats, so they can (say) be transmitted within an email message. Nowadays this is done automatically with attachments and MIME tools, but we'll cover the munpack program, which can do this from the command line.

If you come across a format we don't cover, such as Mac OS X sit files, Arc, Zoo, rar, and others, learn more at *http://en.wikipe dia.org/wiki/List_of_archive_formats*.

---

tar   stdin   stdout   - file   -- opt   --help   --version

`tar [options] [files]`

The tar program packs many files and directories into a single file for easy transport, optionally compressed. (It was originally for backing up files onto a tape drive; its name is short for "tape archive.") Tar files are the most common file-packaging format for Linux.

```
→ tar -czf myarchive.tar.gz mydir          Create
→ ls -lG myarchive.tar.gz
-rw-r--r-- 1 smith 350 Nov  7 14:09 myarchive.tar.gz
→ tar -tf myarchive.tar.gz                 List contents
mydir/
mydir/dir/
mydir/dir/file10
mydir/file1
mydir/file2
...
→ tar -xf myarchive.tar.gz                 Extract
```

If you specify files on the command line, only those files are processed:

→ `tar -xvf myarchive.tar myfile myfile2 myfile3`

Otherwise, the entire archive is processed.

Useful options

`-c`	Create an archive. You'll have to list the input files and directories on the command line.
`-r`	Append files to an existing archive.
`-u`	Append new/changed files to an existing archive.
`-A`	Append one archive to the end of another: for example, `tar -A -f first.tar second.tar` appends the contents of *second.tar* to *first.tar*. Does not work for compressed archives.
`-t`	List (test) the archive.
`-x`	Extract files from the archive.
`-f file`	Read the archive from, or write the archive to, the given file. This is usually a tar file on disk (such as *myarchive.tar*) but can also be a tape drive (such as */dev/tape*).
`-d`	Diff (compare) the archive against the filesystem.
`-z`	Use `gzip` compression.
`-j`	Use `bzip2` compression.
`-Z`	Use Unix compression.
`-v`	Verbose mode: print extra information.
`-h`	Follow symbolic links rather than merely copying them.
`-p`	When extracting files, restore their original permissions and ownership.

---

gzip   stdin   stdout   - file   -- opt   --help   --version

`gzip [options] [files]`

`gunzip [options] [files]`

```
zcat [options] [files]
```

gzip and gunzip compress and uncompress files in GNU Zip format. The original file may be deleted in some cases, as shown. Compressed files have the extension *.gz*.

Sample commands

`gzip file`	Compress *file* to create *file.gz*. Original *file* is deleted.
`gzip -c file`	Produce compressed data on standard output.
`cat file	gzip`	Produce compressed data from a pipeline.
`gunzip file.gz`	Uncompress *file.gz* to create *file*. Original *file.gz* is deleted.
`gunzip -c file.gz`	Uncompress the data on standard output.
`cat file.gz	gunzip`	Uncompress the data from a pipeline.
`zcat file.gz`	Uncompress the data on standard output.
`tar -czf tarfile dir`	Pack directory *dir* into a gzipped tar file. Use -cvzf to print filenames as they are processed.

---

bzip2   stdin   stdout   -file   --opt   --help   --version

```
bzip2 [options] [files]
bunzip2 [options] [files]
bzcat [options] [files]
```

bzip2 and bunzip2 compress and uncompress files in Burrows–Wheeler format. The original file may be deleted in some cases, as shown. Compressed files have the extension *.bz2*.

Sample commands

bzip2 *file*	Compress *file* to create *file.bz2*. Original *file* is deleted.
bzip2 -c *file*	Produce compressed data on standard output.
cat *file* | bzip2	Produce compressed data on standard output.
bunzip2 *file*.bz2	Uncompress *file.bz2* to create *file*. Original *file.bz2* is deleted.
bunzip2 -c *file*.bz2	Uncompress the data on standard output.
cat *file*.bz2 | bunzip2	Uncompress the data on standard output.
bzcat *file*.bz2	Uncompress the data on standard output.
tar -cjf *tarfile dir*	Pack directory *dir* into a bzipped tar file. Use -cvjf to print filenames as they are processed.

---

compress   stdin   stdout   - file   --opt   --help   --version

compress [*options*] [*files*]

uncompress [*options*] [*files*]

zcat [*options*] [*files*]

compress and uncompress compress and uncompress files in standard Unix compression format (Lempel Ziv). The original file may be deleted in some cases, as shown. Compressed files have the extension *.Z*.

Sample commands

compress *file*	Compress *file* to create *file.Z*. Original *file* is deleted.
compress -c *file*	Produce compressed data on standard output.

`cat file	compress`	Produce compressed data from a pipeline.
`uncompress file.Z`	Uncompress `file.Z` to create `file`. Original `file.Z` is deleted.
`uncompress -c file.Z`	Uncompress the data on standard output.
`cat file.Z	uncompress`	Uncompress the data from a pipeline.
`zcat file.Z`	Uncompress the data on standard output.
`tar -cZf tarfile dir`	Pack directory `dir` into a compressed tar file. Use `-cvZf` to print filenames as they are processed.

---

zip   stdin   stdout   - file   -- opt   **--help**   **--version**

`zip [options] [files]`

zip and unzip compress and uncompress files in Windows Zip format. Compressed files have the extension *.zip*. Unlike most other Linux compression commands, zip does not delete the original files.

`zip myfile.zip file1 file2 file3...`	Pack.
`zip -r myfile.zip dirname`	Pack recursively.
`unzip -l myfile.zip`	List contents.
`unzip myfile.zip`	Unpack.

---

munpack   stdin   stdout   - file   **--opt**   --help   --version

`munpack [options] mail_file`

`mpack [options] files`

Modern email programs can send and receive attachments so easily we rarely think about it, but this was not always the case. Programs like munpack were created to work with attachments directly on the command line, appending or extracting them to and from mail messages. For example, if you have an email message in a file, *messagefile*, and it contains a JPEG image and a PDF file as attachments, munpack can extract both attachments as files:

```
→ munpack messagefile
beautiful.jpg (image/jpeg)
researchpaper.pdf (application/pdf)
```

Its partner program, mpack, does the opposite, inserting one or more files as attachments into a MIME-format file. Here we create the file *attachment.mime* containing a MIME-encoded image, *photo.jpg*:

```
→ mpack -o attachment.mime photo.jpg
Subject: My photo
```

File Comparison

diff	Line-by-line comparison of two files or directories.
comm	Line-by-line comparison of two sorted files.
cmp	Byte-by-byte comparison of two files.
md5sum	Compute a checksum of the given files (MD5).

There are three ways to compare Linux files:

- Line by line (diff, diff3, sdiff, comm), best suited to text files
- Byte by byte (cmp), often used for binary files
- By comparing checksums (md5sum, sum, cksum)

```
diff [options] file1 file2
```

The diff command compares two files (or two directories) line by line. When comparing text files, diff can produce detailed reports of their differences. For binary files, diff merely reports whether they differ or not. For all files, if there are no differences, diff produces no output.

The traditional output format looks like this:

Indication of line numbers and the type of change
< *Corresponding section of file1, if any*
- - -
> *Corresponding section of file2, if any*

For example, if we start with a file *fileA*:

```
Hello, this is a wonderful file.
The quick brown fox jumped over
the lazy dogs.
Goodbye for now.
```

Suppose we delete the first line, change "brown" to "blue" on the second line, and add a final line, creating a file *fileB*:

```
The quick blue fox jumped over
the lazy dogs.
Goodbye for now.
Linux r00lz!
```

Then the diff command produces this output for these files:

```
→ diff fileA fileB
1,2c1                                fileA lines 1-2 became fileB line 1
< Hello, this is a wonderful file.    Lines 1-2 of fileA
< The quick brown fox jumped over
---                                   diff separator
> The quick blue fox jumped over      Line 1 of fileB
4a4                                   Line 4 was added in fileB
> Linux r00lz!                        The added line
```

The leading symbols < and > are arrows indicating *fileA* and *fileB*, respectively. This output format is the default: many others are available, some of which can be fed directly to other tools. Try them out to see what they look like.

Option	Output format
-n	RCS version control format, as produced by `rcsdiff` (`man rcsdiff`).
-c	Context diff format, as used by the `patch` command (`man patch`).
-D *macro*	C preprocessor format, using `#ifdef` *macro* ... `#else` ... `#endif`.
-u	Unified format, which merges the files and prepends "-" for deletion and "+" for addition.
-y	Side-by-side format; use `-W` to adjust the width of the output.
-e	Create an ed script that would change *fileA* into *fileB* if run.
-q	Don't report changes, just say whether the files differ.

`diff` can also compare directories:

→ **`diff dir1 dir2`**

which compares any same-named files in those directories, and lists all files that appear in one directory but not the other. To compare entire directory hierarchies recursively, use the `-r` option:

→ **`diff -r dir1 dir2`**

which produces a (potentially massive) report of all differences.

Useful options

- -b   Don't consider whitespace.

- -B   Don't consider blank lines.

- -i   Ignore case.

-r   When comparing directories, recurse into subdirectories.

diff is just one member of a family of programs that operate on file differences. Some others are diff3, which compares three files at a time, and sdiff, which merges the differences between two files to create a third file according to your instructions.

---

comm   stdin   **stdout**   - file   -- opt   --help   --version

comm [*options*] *file1 file2*

The comm command compares two sorted files and produces three columns of output, separated by tabs:

1. All lines that appear in *file1* but not in *file2*.

2. All lines that appear in *file2* but not in *file1*.

3. All lines that appear in both files.

For example, if *commfile1* and *commfile2* contain these lines:

commfile1:	*commfile2:*
apple	baker
baker	charlie
charlie	dark

then comm produces this three-column output:

```
→ comm commfile1 commfile2
apple
                baker
                charlie
        dark
```

Useful options

-1   Suppress column 1.

-2   Suppress column 2.

-3   Suppress column 3.

-23   Show lines that appear only in the first file.

-13   Show lines that appear only in the second file.

-12   Show only common lines.

---

cmp
stdin   stdout -file --opt --help --version

```
cmp [options] file1 file2 [offset1 [offset2]]
```

The cmp command compares two files. If their contents are the same, cmp reports nothing; otherwise, it lists the location of the first difference:

```
→ cmp myfile yourfile
myfile yourfile differ: byte 225, line 4
```

By default, cmp does not tell you what the difference is, only where it is. It also is perfectly suitable for comparing binary files, as opposed to diff, which operates best on text files.

Normally, cmp starts its comparison at the beginning of each file, but it will start elsewhere if you provide offsets:

```
→ cmp myfile yourfile 10 20
```

This begins the comparison at the tenth character of *myfile* and the twentieth of *yourfile*.

Useful options

-l   Long output: print all differences, byte by byte:

```
→ cmp -l myfile yourfile
225 167 127
```

This means at offset 225 (in decimal), *myfile* has a small "w" (octal 167) but *yourfile* has a capital "W" (octal 127).

-s Silent output: don't print anything, just exit with an appropriate return code; 0 if the files match, 1 if they don't. (Or other codes if the comparison fails.)

---

md5sum

stdin   stdout   - file   -- opt   --help   --version

```
md5sum files | --check file
```

The md5sum command works with checksums to verify that files are unchanged. The first form produces the 32-byte checksum of the given files, using the MD5 algorithm:

```
→ md5sum myfile
48760f921ec6111e3979efa14e22535d  myfile
```

while the second form tests whether a checksum matches its file, using --check:

```
→ md5sum myfile myfile2 myfile3 > mysum
→ cat mysum
48760f921ec6111e3979efa14e22535d  myfile
49f6c28a5ec01d15703794a31accd08d  myfile2
d28b9f7fc7d61c60913c8026fc91149a  myfile3
→ md5sum --check mysum
myfile: OK
myfile2: OK
myfile3: OK
→ echo "new data" > myfile2
→ md5sum --check mysum
myfile: OK
myfile2: FAILED
myfile3: OK
md5sum: WARNING: 1 of 3 computed checksums did NOT
match
```

Two different files are highly unlikely to have the same MD5 checksum, so comparing checksums is a reasonably reliable way to detect if two files differ:

```
→ md5sum myfile | cut -c1-32 > sum1
→ md5sum myfile2 | cut -c1-32 > sum2
→ diff -q sum1 sum2
Files sum1 and sum2 differ
```

A stronger but (as yet) less popular program is shasum, which can produce longer hashes using a different algorithm. It is likely more reliable than md5sum.

```
→ shasum myfile                          SHA-1 algorithm
253c9c5836261859a77f83dc296168b35c1230ac  myfile
→ shasum -a 256 myfile                    SHA-256 algorithm
e8183aaa23aa9b74c7033cbc843041fcf1d1e9e93724b7ef63c94d
4c50a15df8 myfile
→ shasum myfile > mysum
→ shasum --check mysum
myfile: OK
```

Avoid older, weaker programs such as sum and cksum which produce much smaller, unreliable checksums.

PDF and PostScript File Handling

pdftotext	Extract text from PDF files.
ps2ascii	Extract text from PostScript or PDF files.
pdfseparate	Extract individual pages from a PDF file.
pdftk	Split, join, rotate, and otherwise manipulate PDF files.
pdf2ps, ps2pdf	Convert between PDF and PostScript file formats.

You may commonly encounter files in Adobe PDF format, especially when exchanging files with Windows or Mac OS X computers. Less commonly, you may encounter files in Post-Script format, or you might need to convert files to PostScript in order to print them. Linux has a rich set of tools for working with PDF and PostScript files, even if you're working in the shell and can't view the files graphically.

If you simply want to display PDF and PostScript files, you have a number of choices. The commands evince, okular, and

---

gv (Ghostview) all display both types of files, and xpdf displays only PDFs. There's also a full-featured but ancient "official" PDF viewer from Adobe, acroread, but it is no longer maintained and is relatively slow. All of these programs are available on the command line. For more complex handling of PDF and PostScript files, read on.

---

pdftotext

stdin   stdout   **- file**   **-- opt**   **--help**   --version

pdftotext [*options*] [*file*.pdf [*outfile*.txt]]

The pdftotext command extracts text from a PDF file and writes it to a file. This works only if the PDF contains actual text, not images that look like text (say, a magazine article that's been scanned on a graphical scanner).

→ **pdftotext sample.pdf**   *Creates sample.txt*

Useful options

-f *N*	Begin with page *N* of the PDF file. You must have a space between the option and the number.
-l *N*	End with page *N* of the PDF file. You must have a space between the option and the number.
-htmlmeta	Generate HTML rather than plain text.
-eol (dos | mac | unix)	Write end-of-line characters in the text file for the given operating system.

ps2ascii

```
ps2ascii file.(ps|pdf)] [outfile.txt]
```

The ps2ascii command extracts text from a PostScript file. It's a simple command with no options.[13] To extract text from *sample.ps* and place it into *extracted.txt*:

> → **ps2ascii sample.ps extracted.txt**

ps2ascii can also extract text from a PDF file, though you wouldn't guess that from the command name.[14]

> → **ps2ascii sample.pdf extracted.txt**

pdfseparate

```
pdfseparate [options] [file.pdf] [pattern.txt]
```

The pdfseparate command splits a PDF file into separate PDF files, one per page. For example, if *one.pdf* is 10 pages long, then this command will create 10 PDF files named *split1.pdf* through *split10.pdf*, each containing one page:

> → **pdfseparate one.pdf split%d.pdf**

The final argument is a pattern for forming the names of the individual page files. The special notation %d stands for the extracted page number.

---

13 Actually, if you run ps2ascii --help, you'll be presented with command-line options, but they don't work. They are the options of a related program, gs, which gets invoked by ps2ascii.

14 At press time, the manpage for ps2ascii says that the PDF file cannot come from standard input, but in practice it seems to work fine: cat sample.pdf | ps2ascii.

Useful options

- -f *N*   Begin with page *N* of the PDF file. You must have a space between the option and the number.

- -l *N*   End with page *N* of the PDF file. You must have a space between the option and the number.

---

pdftk   stdin   stdout   -file   --opt   --help   --version

```
pdftk [arguments]
```

pdftk is the "Swiss Army knife" of PDF commands. This versatile program can extract pages from a PDF file, join several PDFs into one, rotate pages, add watermarks, encrypt and decrypt files, and much more, all from the command line. This power comes with complicated syntax, unfortunately, but with a little effort you can learn a few useful tricks.

To join the files *one.pdf* and *two.pdf* into a single PDF file, *combined.pdf*:

```
→ pdftk one.pdf two.pdf cat output combined.pdf
```

To extract pages 5, 7, and 10–15 from the file *one.pdf* and write them to *new.pdf*:

```
→ pdftk one.pdf cat 5 7 10-15 output new.pdf
```

Extract the first five pages from *one.pdf* and the odd-numbered pages from *two.pdf* and combine them as *combined.pdf*:

```
→ pdftk A=one.pdf B=two.pdf cat A1-5 Bodd output \
  combined.pdf
```

Copy the file *one.pdf* to *new.pdf*, but with page 7 rotated by 90 degrees clockwise ("east"):

```
→ pdftk one.pdf cat 1-6 7east 8-end output new.pdf
```

Interleave the pages of *one.pdf* and *two.pdf*, creating *interleaved.pdf*:

```
→ pdftk one.pdf two.pdf shuffle output \
  interleaved.pdf
```

You may have noticed that the page selection criteria, typically appearing before the output keyword, are very powerful. They consist of one or more page ranges with qualifiers. A page range can be a single page like 5, a range like 5-10, or a reverse range like 10-5 (which will reverse the pages in the output). Qualifiers can remove pages from a range, like 1-100~20-25, which means "all pages from 1 to 100 except for pages 20 to 25." They can also specify only odd pages or even pages, using the keywords odd or even, and rotations using the compass directions north, south, east, and west. We've only scratched the surface of pdftk's abilities. The manpage has many more examples and full syntax.

---

pdf2ps   stdin   stdout   **-file**   --opt   **--help**   --version

```
pdf2ps [options] file.pdf [file.ps]
```

```
ps2pdf [options] file.ps [file.pdf]
```

The pdf2ps command converts an Adobe PDF file into a PostScript file (if you don't provide an output file name, the default is to use the input filename, with *.pdf* replaced by *.ps*):

```
→ pdf2ps sample.pdf converted.ps
```

The command has a couple of options but they are rarely used. See the manpage if you're interested.

To go in the opposite direction, converting a PostScript file to PDF format, use ps2pdf:

```
→ ps2pdf sample.ps converted.pdf
```

Printing

lpr   Print a file.

lpq   View the print queue.

lprm   Remove a print job from the queue.

Linux has two popular printing systems, called CUPS and LPRng. Both systems use commands with the same names: lpr, lpq, and lprm. However, these commands have different options depending on whether you're using CUPS or LPRng. To be generally helpful, we will present common options that work with both systems.

In the past, installing a printer on Linux required editing a cryptic configuration file, such as */etc/cups/printers.conf* or */etc/printcap*. Nowadays, both GNOME and KDE have printer configuration tools in their system settings that generate these files.

To troubleshoot a CUPS printer, visit *http://localhost:631* to access your computer's CUPS management system.

---

lpr
stdin   stdout   - file   -- opt   --help   --version

lpr [*options*] [*files*]

The lpr (line printer) command sends a file to a printer:

→ **lpr -P myprinter myfile**

Useful options

-P *printername*	Send the file to printer *printername*, which you have previously set up.
-# *N*	Print *N* copies of the file.
-J *name*	Set the job *name* that prints on the cover page (if your system is set up to print cover pages).

---

lpq

```
lpq [options]
```

The lpq (line printer queue) command lists all print jobs waiting to be printed.

Useful options

-P *printername*	List the queue for printer *printername*.
-a	List the queue for all printers.
-l	Be verbose: display information in a longer format.

---

lprm

```
lprm [options] [job_IDs]
```

The lprm (line printer remove) command cancels one or more print jobs. Use lpq to learn the ID of the desired print jobs (say, 61 and 78), then type:

→ **lprm -P *printername* 61 78**

If you don't supply any job IDs, your current print job is canceled. (Only the superuser can cancel other users' jobs.) The -P option specifies which print queue contains the job.

Spellchecking

look	Look up the spelling of a word quickly.
aspell	Interactive spelling checker.
spell	Batch spelling checker.

Linux has several spellcheckers built in. If you're accustomed to graphical spellcheckers, you might find Linux's text-based ones fairly primitive, but they can be used in pipelines, which is quite powerful.

---

look

stdin   **stdout**   - file   **-- opt**   --help   --version

look [*options*] *prefix* [*dictionary_file*]

The look command prints (on standard output) words that begin with a given string *prefix*. The words are located in a dictionary file (default */usr/share/dict/words*):

→ **look bigg**
bigger
biggest
Biggs

If you supply your own dictionary file—any text file with alphabetically sorted lines—look will print all lines beginning with the given *prefix*.

Useful options

- f   Ignore case.

- t *X*   Match the prefix only up to and including the termination character *X*. For instance, look -t i big prints all words beginning with "bi".

aspell

```
aspell [options] file | command
```

aspell is an interactive spellchecker. It identifies words that it doesn't recognize and presents alternatives. A few useful commands are:

aspell -c *file*
> Interactively check, and optionally correct, the spelling of all words in file.

aspell dump master
> Print aspell's master dictionary on standard output.

aspell help
> Print a concise help message. See *http://aspell.net* for more information.

spell

```
spell [files]
```

The spell command prints all words in the given files that are misspelled, according to its dictionary (it is not interactive):

```
→ cat badwords
This Linux file has some spelling errors.
You may naturaly wonder if a spelling checker
will pick them up. Careful Linuxx users should
run thier favorite spelling checker on this file.
→ spell badwords
naturaly
Linuxx
thier
```

Disks and Filesystems

df   Display available space on mounted filesystems.

mount   Make a disk partition accessible.

umount   Unmount a disk partition (make it inaccessible).

fsck   Check a disk partition for errors.

eject   Eject a CD, DVD, or other removable disk.

Linux systems can have multiple disks or disk partitions. In casual conversation, these are variously called disks, partitions, filesystems, volumes, even directories. We'll try to be more accurate.

A *disk* is a hardware device, which may be divided into *partitions* that act as independent storage devices. Partitions are represented on Linux systems as special files in (usually) the directory */dev*. For example, */dev/sda7* could be a partition on your hard drive. Some common devices in */dev* are:

sda   First block device, such as SCSI, SATA, USB, or FireWire hard drives;
          partitions are *sda1*, *sda2*, ...

sdb   Second block device; partitions are *sdb1*, *sdb2*, ... Likewise for *sdc*, *sdd*, ...

scd0   First SCSI CD-ROM drive (then *scd1*, *scd2*, ...)

Before a partition can hold files, it is "formatted" by a program that writes a *filesystem* on it (see "Partitioning and Formatting" on page 132). A filesystem defines how files are represented; examples are ext3 (a Linux journaling filesystem) and ntfs (Microsoft Windows NT filesystem). Formatting is generally done for you when you install Linux.

Once a filesystem is created, you can make it available for use by *mounting* it on an empty directory.[15] For example, if you mount a Windows filesystem on a directory */mnt/win*, it becomes part of your system's directory tree, and you can create and edit files like */mnt/win/myfile*. Mounting is generally done automatically at boot time. Filesystems can also be unmounted to make them inaccessible via the filesystem, say, for maintenance.

Partitioning and Formatting

Disk-related operations like partitioning and formatting can be complex on Linux systems. Here are pointers to the programs you may need (start with their manpages):

gparted, parted, fdisk, *or* sfdisk
    Partition a hard drive. Any of these programs will work in most cases. gparted has the simplest user interface.

mkfs
    Format a hard disk (i.e., create a new filesystem).

---

df   stdin   **stdout**   - file   **-- opt**   **--help**   **--version**

df [*options*] [*disk devices* | *files* | *directories*]

The df (disk free) program shows you the size, used space, and free space on a given disk partition. If you supply a file or directory, df describes the disk device on which that file or directory resides. With no arguments, df reports on all mounted filesystems:

---

15 You can mount a filesystem on a nonempty directory, but the directory's contents will become inaccessible until you unmount.

```
→ df
Filesystem 1k-blocks     Used    Avail Use% Mounted on
/dev/sda    1011928    225464   735060  24% /
/dev/sda9    521748    249148   246096  51% /var
/dev/sda8   8064272   4088636  3565984  54% /usr
/dev/sda10  8064272   4586576  3068044  60% /home
```

Useful options

- `-k`   List sizes in kilobytes (the default).

- `-m`   List sizes in megabytes.

- `-B N`   Display sizes in blocks of N bytes. (Default = 1024)

- `-h`   Print human-readable output, and choose the most appropriate unit
- `-H`   for each size. For example, if your two disks have 1 gigabyte and 25
             kilobytes free, respectively, df -h prints 1G and 25K. The -h option
             uses powers of 1024, whereas -H uses powers of 1000.

- `-l`   Display only local filesystems, not networked filesystems.

- `-T`   Include the filesystem type (ext3, vfat, etc.) in the output.

- `-t type` Display only filesystems of the given type.

- `-x type` Don't display filesystems of the given type.

- `-i`   Inode mode. Display total, used, and free inodes for each filesystem,
             instead of disk blocks.

---

mount   stdin   **stdout**   - file   -- opt   **--help**   **--version**

```
mount [options] device | directory
```

The mount command makes a partition accessible. Most commonly it handles disk drives (say, */dev/sda1*) and removable media (e.g., USB keys), making them accessible via an existing directory (say, */mnt/mydir*):

```
→ sudo mkdir /mnt/mydir
→ ls /mnt/mydir                    Notice it's empty
→ sudo mount /dev/sda1 /mnt/mydir
→ ls /mnt/mydir
file1  file2  file3      Files on the mounted partition
→ df /mnt/mydir
Filesystem 1K-blocks   Used  Avail Use% Mounted on
/dev/sda1   1011928 285744 674780  30% /mnt/mydir
```

mount has tons of options and uses; we will discuss only the most basic.

In most common cases, mount reads the file */etc/fstab* (filesystem table) to learn how to mount a desired disk. For example, if you type mount /usr, the mount command looks up "/usr" in */etc/fstab*, whose line might look like this:

```
/dev/sda8    /usr    ext3    defaults    1    2
```

Here mount learns, among other things, that disk device */dev/sda8* should be mounted on */usr* as a Linux ext3-formatted filesystem. Now you can mount */dev/sda8* on */usr* with either of these commands:

```
→ sudo mount /dev/sda8       By device
→ sudo mount /usr            By directory
```

mount is run typically by the superuser, but common removable devices like USB keys and DVDs often can be mounted and unmounted by any user.

Useful options

-t *type* Specify the type of filesystem, such as ext3 or ntfs.

-l   List all mounted filesystems; works with -t too.

-a   Mount all filesystems listed in */etc/fstab*. Ignores entries that include the noauto option. Works well with -t too.

-r   Mount the filesystem read-only (but see the manpage for some disclaimers).

umount stdin **stdout** -file **--opt** --help --version

```
umount [options] [device | directory]
```

umount does the opposite of mount: it makes a disk partition unavailable via the filesystem.[16] For instance, if you've mounted a DVD, you can't eject it until it's umounted:

→ **umount "/media/smith/My Vacation Photos"**

Always unmount a removable medium before ejecting it, particularly if it's writable, or you risk damage to its filesystem. To unmount all mounted devices:

→ **sudo umount -a**

Don't unmount a filesystem that's in use; in fact, the umount command will refuse to do so for safety reasons.

---

fsck stdin **stdout** -file **--opt** --help --version

```
fsck [options] [devices]
```

The fsck (filesystem check) command validates a Linux disk partition and, if requested, repairs errors found on it. fsck is run automatically when your system boots; however, you can run it manually if you like. In general, unmount a device before checking it, so no other programs are operating on it at the same time:

```
→ sudo umount /dev/sda10
→ sudo fsck -f /dev/sda10
Pass 1: Checking inodes, blocks, and sizes
Pass 2: Checking directory structure
Pass 3: Checking directory connectivity
```

---

16 Notice the spelling is "umount," not "unmount."

```
Pass 4: Checking reference counts
Pass 5: Checking group summary information
/home: 172/1281696 files (11.6% non-contiguous), ...
```

You cannot use fsck to fix your root filesystem while your system is running normally. You'll need to boot first on a Linux CD, DVD, or other rescue media.

fsck is a frontend for a set of filesystem-checking programs found in */sbin*, with names beginning "fsck". Only certain types of filesystems are supported; you can list them with the command:

```
→ ls /sbin/fsck.* | cut -d. -f2
```

Useful options

- -A Check all disks listed in */etc/fstab*, in order.

- -N Print a description of the checking that would be done, but exit without performing any checking.

- -r Fix errors interactively, prompting before each fix.

- -a Fix errors automatically (use only if you *really* know what you're doing; if not, you can seriously mess up a filesystem).

---

eject   stdin   stdout   - file   -- opt   --help   --version

```
eject [options] [device_name]
```

The eject command does the same thing as pressing the open/close button on a removable drive, such as a CD-ROM or DVD drive. It's handy for ejecting a disc when you're physically away from the computer. Of course, the media must be in a state where ejection is possible.

```
→ eject
```

Useful options

-h   Display a help message.

-n   Don't eject anything, just say what would be done. Combine with -v for a detailed description.

-v   Produce verbose output.

-d   Print the name of the default device to be ejected, such as /dev/cdrom, and exit.

-c *N*   Eject disc *N* from a multi-disc changer.

Backups and Remote Storage

rsync   Efficiently copy a set of files, even across a network.

dd   Low-level copying of data.

growisofs   Burn a DVD or Blu-ray disc.

There are various way to back up your precious Linux files:

- Copy them to a backup medium, such as an external hard drive.
- Burn them onto a writable CD, DVD, or Blu-ray disc.
- Mirror them to a remote machine.

We aren't presenting every available Linux command for backups. Some users prefer cpio for its flexibility, and some longtime administrators swear by dump and restore as the only reliable way to back up every type of file. See the manpages for these programs if you are interested in them.

```
rsync [options] source destination
```

The rsync command copies a set of files. It can make an exact copy, including file permissions and other attributes (called *mirroring*), or it can just copy the data. It can run over a network or on a single machine. rsync has many uses and over 50 options; we'll present just a few common cases relating to backups.

To mirror the directory *mydir* and its contents into another directory *mydir2* on a single machine:

```
→ rsync -a mydir mydir2
```

rsync is finicky about how you specify the first directory. If you write mydir as in the example here, that directory will be copied *into mydir2*, creating *mydir2/mydir*. That might not be what you want. If you'd rather have the *contents* of *mydir* copied into *mydir2*, append a slash onto mydir:

```
→ rsync -a mydir/ mydir2
```

In order to mirror directory *mydir* over the network to another host, *server.example.com*, where you have an account with username "smith." rsync automatically secures the connection with SSH to prevent eavesdropping:

```
→ rsync -a mydir smith@server.example.com:D2
```

If you like working with rsync but want to have incremental backups and manage them efficiently, look into rsnapshot (*http://rsnapshot.org/*).

Useful options

- -o   Copy the ownership of the files. (You might need superuser privileges on the remote host.)

- -g Copy the group ownership of the files. (You might need superuser privileges on the remote host.)

- -p Copy the file permissions.

- -t Copy the file timestamps.

- -r Copy directories recursively (i.e., including their contents).

- -l Permit symbolic links to be copied (not the files they point to).

- -D Permit devices to be copied. (Superuser only.)

- -a Mirroring: copy all attributes of the original files. This implies all of the options -ogptrlD.

- -x When copying a tree of files, remain within the current filesystem; do not cross over into other mounted filesystems.

- -n Dry-run mode: don't actually do any copying. Just display what *would* be done.

- -v Verbose mode: print information about what's happening during the copy. Add - -progress to display a numeric progress meter while files are copied.

---

dd   **stdin** **stdout** -file --opt **--help** **--version**

dd [*options*]

dd is a low-level copier of bits and bytes. It can copy data from one file to another, say, from *file1* to *file2*:

```
→ dd if=fileA of=fileC
7+1 records in
7+1 records out
3816 bytes (3.8 kB) copied, 0.000356028 s, 10.7 MB/s
```

and it can even perform data conversions while it copies. For example, you can convert all characters to uppercase as you transfer data between files:

```
→ dd if=fileA of=filecaps conv=ucase
7+1 records in
7+1 records out
3816 bytes (3.8 kB) copied, 0.000389499 s, 9.8 MB/s
```

dd does much more than copying files, however. It can clone a disk by copying from one device to another (*Warning! This will DESTROY all data on the destination device!*):

```
→ sudo dd if=/dev/device1 of=/dev/device2 bs=512 \
  conv=noerror,sync
```

dd is simple in the sense that it does one thing very well—moving bits—but it's also complex because if you're not careful, you can *wipe out your hard drive* in seconds. Back up your computer and keep a Linux "live" DVD on hand (see "What's in This Book?" on page 1) before playing around with dd as the superuser.

Visit *https://wiki.archlinux.org/index.php/Disk_cloning* for some great advice on sophisticated uses of dd. My favorite is copying just the master boot record (MBR) from a disk, where the MBR is 512 bytes long, to a file called *mybootrecord*:

```
→ sudo dd if=/dev/device of=mybootrecord bs=512 \
  count=1
```

Useful options

if=*file*	Specify an input file or device.
of=*file*	Specify an output file or device.
bs=*N*	Copy *N* bytes at a time, known as the "block size." (To set the block size differently for the input and the output, use ibs and obs, respectively.)
skip=*N*	Skip past *N* blocks of input before starting the copy.
seek=*N*	Discard *N* blocks of output before starting the copy.

conv=*spec*   Convert the data being copied. *spec* can be ucase (convert to
          uppercase), lcase (convert to lowercase), ascii (convert to
          ASCII from EBCDIC), and many others listed on the manpage.

---

growisofs   stdin   stdout   - file   -- opt   --help   --version

growisofs [*options*] *tracks*

The growisofs command burns a writable CD, DVD, or Blu-
ray disc. To burn the contents of a Linux directory onto a disc
readable on Linux, Windows, and Mac OS X systems:

1. Locate your disc writer's device by running:

   ```
   → more /proc/sys/dev/cdrom/info
   CD-ROM information, Id: cdrom.c 3.20 2003/12/17

   drive name:            sr1     sr0
   drive speed:           48      12
   drive # of slots:      1       1
   Can close tray:        1       1
   Can open tray:         1       1
   ...
   ```

   The available devices here are */dev/sr1* and */dev/sr0*.

2. Put the files you want to burn into a directory, say, *dir*.
   Arrange them exactly as you'd like them on the disc. The
   directory *dir* itself will not be copied to the disc, just its
   contents.

3. Use the mkisofs command to create an ISO (disc) image
   file, and burn it onto a disc using growisofs, assuming
   your device is */dev/sr1*:

   ```
   → mkisofs -R -l -o $HOME/mydisk.iso dir
   → growisofs -dvd-compat -Z /dev/sr1=$HOME/mydisk.iso
   → rm $HOME/mydisk.iso
   ```

If you want to burn audio CDs, use a friendlier, graphical program like k3b instead.

Viewing Processes

ps	List process.
uptime	View the system load.
w	List active processes for all users.
top	Monitor resource-intensive processes interactively.
free	Display free memory.

A *process* is a unit of work on a Linux system. Each program you run represents one or more processes, and Linux provides commands for viewing and manipulating them. Every process is identified by a numeric *process ID*, or PID.

Processes are different from jobs (see "Shell Job Control" on page 39): processes are part of the operating system, whereas jobs are higher-level constructs known only to the shell in which they're running. A running program comprises one or more processes; a job consists of one or more programs executed as a shell command.

---

ps   stdin   **stdout**   - file   -- opt   **--help**   **--version**

ps [*options*]

The ps command displays information about your running processes, and optionally the processes of other users:

```
→ ps
  PID TTY          TIME CMD
 4706 pts/2    00:00:01 bash
15007 pts/2    00:00:00 emacs
16729 pts/2    00:00:00 ps
```

ps has at least 80 options; we'll cover just a few useful combinations. If the options seem arbitrary or inconsistent, it's because the supplied ps command (GNU ps) incorporates the features of several other Unix ps commands, attempting to be compatible with all of them.

To view your processes:

→ **ps -ux**

all of user "smith's" processes:

→ **ps -U smith**

all occurrences of a program:

→ **ps -C** *program_name*

processes on terminal *N*:

→ **ps -t***N*

particular processes 1, 2, and 3505:

→ **ps -p1,2,3505**

all processes with command lines truncated to screen width:

→ **ps -ef**

all processes with full command lines:

→ **ps -efww**

and all processes in a threaded view, which indents child processes below their parents:

→ **ps -efH**

Remember, you can extract information more finely from the output of ps using grep and other filter programs:

→ **ps -ux | grep myprogram**

uptime   stdin   **stdout**   - file   -- opt   --help   --version

uptime

The uptime command tells you how long the system has been
running since the last boot:

```
→ uptime
  10:54pm up 8 days, 3:44, 3 users,
  load average: 0.89, 1.00, 2.15
```

This information is, from beginning to end: the current time
(10:54pm), system uptime (8 days, 3 hours, 44 minutes), number of users logged in (3), and system load average for three
time periods: one minute (0.89), five minutes (1.00), and fifteen
minutes (2.15). The load average is the average number of processes ready to run in that time interval.

---

w   stdin   **stdout**   - file   **-- opt**   --help   --version

w [*username*]

The w command displays the current process running in each
shell for all logged-in users:

```
→ w
  10:51pm  up 8 days,  3:42,  8 users,
  load average: 2.02, 3.79, 5.44
 USER    TTY  FROM   LOGIN@   IDLE   JCPU   PCPU  WHAT
 barrett pts/0 :0    Sat 2pm 27:13m 0.07s  0.07s emacs
 jones   pts/1 host1 6Sep03   2:33m 0.74s  0.21s bash
 smith   pts/2 host2 6Sep03   0.00s 13.35s 0.04s w
```

The top line is the same one printed by uptime. The columns
indicate the user's terminal, originating host or X display (if
applicable), login time, idle time, two measures of the CPU
time (run man w for details), and the current process. Provide a
username to see only that user's information.

For the briefest output, try w -hfs.

Useful options

- -h Don't print the header line.

- -f Don't print the FROM column.

- -s Don't print the JCPU and PCPU columns.

---

top   stdin   **stdout**   - file   -- opt   --help   --version

```
top [options]
```

The top command lets you monitor the most active processes, updating the display at regular intervals (say, every second). It is a screen-based program that updates the display in place, interactively:

```
→ top
94 processes: 81 sleeping, 1 running, 0 zombie,
  11 stopped
CPU states: 1.1% user, 0.5% system, 0.0% nice,
  4.5% idle
Mem: 523812K av, 502328K used, 21484K free, ...
Swap:  530104K av,  0K used, 530104K free
  115300K cached

PID   USER PRI NI SIZE SHARE STAT %CPU %MEM TIME CMD
26265 smith 10 0 1092  840   R    4.7  0.2  0:00 top
    1 root   0 0  540  472   S    0.0  0.1  0:07 init
  914 www    0 0    0    0   SW   0.0  0.0  0:00 httpd
...
```

While top is running, you can press keys to change its behavior, such as setting the update speed (s), hiding idle processes (i), or killing processes (k). Type h to see a complete list and q to quit. For similar programs to monitor your system's I/O and network bandwidth, try iotop and iftop.

Useful options

-n*N*	Perform *N* updates, then quit.
-d*N*	Update the display every *N* seconds.
-p*N* -p*M* ...	Display only the processes with PID *N, M, ...,* up to 20 processes.
-c	Display the command-line arguments of processes.
-b	Print on standard output noninteractively, without playing screen tricks. top -b -n1 > outfile saves a quick snapshot to a file.

---

free

free [*options*]

The free command displays memory usage in kilobytes:

```
→ free
        total      used     free shared buffers cached
Mem:   523812    491944    31868      0   67856 199276
-/+ buffers/cache: 224812  299000
Swap: 530104        0   530104
```

The Linux kernel reserves as much memory as possible for caching purposes, so your best estimate of free RAM in the preceding output is in the buffers/cache row, free column (i.e., 299000K).

Useful options

-s *N*	Run continuously and update the display every *N* seconds.
-b	Display amounts in bytes.
-m	Display amounts in megabytes.
-t	Add a totals row at the bottom.
-o	Don't display the "buffers/cache" row.

Controlling Processes

kill	Terminate a process (or send it a signal).
timeout	Kill a command that runs for too long.
nice	Invoke a program at a particular priority.
renice	Change a process's priority as it runs.
flock	Ensure that only one copy of a process runs at the same time, using locks.

Once processes are started, they can be stopped, restarted, killed, and reprioritized. We discussed some of these operations as handled by the shell in "Shell Job Control" on page 39. Now we cover killing and reprioritizing.

---

kill   stdin **stdout** - file -- opt --help --version

kill [*options*] [*process_ids*]

The kill command sends a signal to a process. This can terminate a process (the default action), interrupt it, suspend it, crash it, and so on. You must own the process, or be the superuser, to affect it. To terminate process 13243, for example, run:

→ **kill 13243**

If this does not work—some programs catch this signal without terminating—add the -KILL or (equivalently) -9 option:

→ **kill -KILL 13243**

which is virtually guaranteed to work. However, this is not a clean exit for the program, which may leave resources allocated (or cause other inconsistencies) upon its death.

If you don't know the PID of a process, run ps and examine the output:

```
→ ps -uax | grep emacs
```

or even better, try the pidof command, which looks up and prints the PID of a process by its name:

```
→ pidof emacs
8374
```

Now you can kill a process knowing only its program name in a single line, using shell backquotes to execute pidof:

```
→ kill `pidof emacs`
```

Or use the killall command to kill all processes for a given program:

```
→ killall emacs
```

In addition to the kill program in the filesystem (usually */bin/ kill*), most shells have built-in kill commands, but their syntax and behavior differ. However, they all support the following usage:

```
→ kill -N PID
→ kill -NAME PID
```

where *N* is a signal number, and *NAME* is a signal name without its leading "SIG" (e.g., use -HUP to send the SIGHUP signal). To see a complete list of signals transmitted by kill, run kill -l, though its output differs depending on which kill you're running. For descriptions of the signals, run man 7 signal.

---

timeout   stdin   stdout   - file   -- opt   **--help**   **--version**

```
timeout [options] seconds command...
```

The timeout command sets a time limit for running another program, in seconds. If the program runs longer than the limit, timeout kills it. As a demonstration, here is a sleep command that should run for a minute but gets killed after 3 seconds:

| → `sleep 60` | *Runs for 60 seconds* |
| → `timeout 3 sleep 60` | *Killed after 3 seconds* |

As a more practical example, play music from your MP3 collection for an hour, then stop:

→ `timeout 3600 mplayer *.mp3`

Useful options

| `-s` *signal* | Send a signal other than the default (TERM). The choices are the same ones listed by `kill -l`. |
| `-k` *seconds* | If the program doesn't die after the first signal, wait this many seconds longer and send a deadly KILL signal. |

| **nice** | stdin | **stdout** | - file | -- opt | **--help** | **--version** |

`nice [-n` *level*`]` *command_line*

When invoking a system-intensive program, you can be nice to the other processes (and users) by lowering its priority. That's what the `nice` command is for: it sets a *nice level* (an amount of "niceness") for a process so it gets less attention from the Linux process scheduler.[17] Here's an example of setting a big job to run at nice level 7:

→ `nice -n 7 sort hugefile > outfile`

If you run `nice` without a level, 10 is used. Normal processes (run without `nice`) run at level zero, which you can see by running `nice` with no arguments:

→ `nice`
`0`

---

17 This is called "nicing" the process. You'll hear the term used as a verb: "That process was niced to 12."

The superuser can also lower the nice level, increasing a process's priority:

```
→ sudo nice -n -10 myprogram
```

To see the nice levels of your jobs, use ps and look at the "NI" column:

```
→ ps -o pid,user,args,nice
```

---

renice   stdin **stdout** - file -- opt --help --version

```
renice [-n N] [options] PID
```

While the nice command can invoke a program at a given nice level, renice changes the nice level of an already-running process. Here we increase the nice level (decrease the priority) of process 28734 by five:

```
→ renice -n 5 -p 28734
```

As a quick (though trivial) test, you can create a process that just sleeps for 2 minutes, run it in the background, and change its priority:

```
→ sleep 120 &
→ pidof sleep
2673
→ renice -n 5 -p 2673
2673 (process ID) old priority 0, new priority 5
```

Ordinary users can increase the nice level of their own processes, while the superuser can also decrease it (increasing the priority) and can operate on any process. The valid range is −20 to +20, but avoid high negative numbers or you might interfere with vital system processes.

Useful options

-p *pid*   Affect the given process ID. You can omit the -p and just
            provide a PID (renice -n 5 28734).

-u *username*   Affect all processes owned by the given user.

---

flock   **stdin** **stdout** - file -- opt **--help** **--version**

flock [*options*] *lockfile command...*

Do you ever need to ensure that only one copy of a program runs at a time on your computer? For example, if you run automatic backups every hour using a command like rsync, there's a slight chance that a previous backup might still be running when the next backup launches. The flock command solves this sort of problem. It prevents a command, such as a backup script, from running concurrently with itself. If you try to run two copies of the command at once, the second will fail. For example, this rsync command, when run with flock, will instantly fail if another instance of the same command is already running:

→ **flock -n /tmp/mylock rsync** …

To see flock in action, open two shell windows and run the following command in each shell, one at a time (we'll use the sleep command as a demonstration, which does nothing but wait for a given number of seconds):

→ **flock -n /tmp/mylock sleep 60**

The first command will run, and the second will instantly terminate. The two commands needn't be identical, but they must refer to the same *lockfile* as the first argument. This can be the name of any file or directory, which flock treats as a unique marker to prevent any other commands from running. For example, if you run the same sleep command in one shell and a different command such as `ls` in another, with the same lock file:

```
→ flock -n /tmp/mylock ls
```

the second will still fail. But if you provide different lock files, both commands will run.

Useful options

-n	Instantly fail if another command is already running.
-w *N*	Fail after waiting *N* seconds, if another command is already running.
-s	Use a shared lock instead of an exclusive lock. You can run multiple commands simultaneously with this option, but `flock` will fail if you omit the option. This is useful for permitting a limited number of commands to run simultaneously.

Scheduling Jobs

sleep	Wait a set number of seconds, doing nothing.
watch	Run a program at set intervals.
at	Schedule a job for a single, future time.
crontab	Schedule jobs for many future times.

If you need to launch programs at particular times or at regular intervals, Linux provides several scheduling tools at various degrees of complexity.

---

sleep   stdin   stdout   - file   -- opt   **--help**   **--version**

sleep *time_specification*

The `sleep` command simply waits a set amount of time. The given time specification can be an integer (meaning seconds)

---

or an integer followed by the letter s (also seconds), m (minutes), h (hours), or d (days). For example:

→ **sleep 5m**   *Do nothing for 5 minutes*

sleep is useful for delaying a command for a set amount of time:

→ **sleep 10 && echo 'Ten seconds have passed.'**
(10 seconds pass)
Ten seconds have passed.

---

watch   stdin   **stdout**   - file   -- **opt**   --**help**   --**version**

watch [*options*] *command*

The watch program executes a given command at regular intervals; the default is every two seconds. The command is passed to the shell (so be sure to quote or escape any special characters), and the results are displayed in a full-screen mode, so you can observe the output conveniently and see what has changed. For example, watch -n 60 date executes the date command once a minute, sort of a poor man's clock. Type ^C to exit.

Useful options

-n *seconds*	Set the time between executions, in seconds.
-d	Highlight differences in the output, to emphasize what has changed from one execution to the next.
-g	Exit when the command produces output that is different from the previous execution.

at [*options*] *time_specification*

The at command runs a shell command once at a specified time:

```
→ at 7am next sunday
at> echo Remember to go shopping | mail smith
at> lpr $HOME/shopping-list
at> ^D
<EOT>
job 559 at 2015-09-14 21:30
```

The time specifications understood by at are enormously flexible. In general, you can specify:

- A time followed by a date (not a date followed by a time)
- Only a date (assumes the current clock time)
- Only a time (assumes the very next occurrence, whether today or tomorrow)
- A special word like now, midnight, or teatime (16:00)
- Any of the preceding followed by an offset, like "+ 3 days"

Dates are acceptable in many forms: december 25 2015, 25 december 2015, december 25, 25 december, 12/25/2015, 25.12.2015, 20151225, today, thursday, next thursday, next month, next year, and more. Month names can be abbreviated to three letters (jan, feb, mar, ...). Times are also flexible: 8pm, 8 pm, 8:00pm, 8:00 pm, 20:00, and 2000 are equivalent. Offsets are a plus or minus sign followed by whitespace and an amount of time: + 3 seconds, + 2 weeks, - 1 hour, and so on.[18]

---

18 Programmers can read the precise syntax in */usr/share/doc/at/time-spec*.

If you don't specify a part of the date or time, at copies the missing information from the system date and time. So "next year" means one year from right now, "thursday" means the upcoming Thursday at the current clock time, "december 25" means the next upcoming December 25, and "4:30pm" means the very next occurrence of 4:30 p.m. in the future.

The command you supply to at is not evaluated by the shell until execution time, so wildcards, variables, and other shell constructs are not expanded until then. Also, your current environment (see printenv) is preserved within each job so it executes as if you were logged in. Aliases, however, aren't available to at jobs, so don't include them.

To list your at jobs, use atq ("at queue"):

```
→ atq
559   2015-09-14 07:00 a smith
```

To delete an at job, run atrm ("at remove") with the job number:

```
→ atrm 559
```

Useful options

-f *filename*   Read commands from the given file instead of standard input.

-c *job_number*   Print the job commands to standard output.

---

crontab   stdin   **stdout**   - **file**   -- **opt**   --help   --version

```
crontab [options] [file]
```

The crontab command, like the at command, schedules jobs for specific times. However, crontab is for recurring jobs, such as "Run this command at midnight on the second Tuesday of each month." To make this work, you edit and save a file (called

---

your *crontab file*), which automatically gets installed in a system directory (*/var/spool/cron*). Once a minute, a Linux process called cron wakes up, checks your crontab file, and executes any jobs that are due.

→ **crontab -e**

Edit your crontab file in your default editor ($VISUAL).

→ **crontab -l**

Print your crontab file on standard output.

→ **crontab -r**

Delete your crontab file.

→ **crontab myfile**

Install the file *myfile* as your crontab file.

The superuser can add the option -u *username* to work with other users' crontab files.

Crontab files contain one job per line. (Blank lines and comment lines beginning with "#" are ignored.) Each line has six fields, separated by whitespace. The first five fields specify the time to run the job, and the last is the job command itself.

Minutes of the hour

Integers between 0 and 59. This can be a single number (30), a sequence of numbers separated by commas (0,15,30,45), a range (20-30), a sequence of ranges (0-15,50-59), or an asterisk to mean "all." You can also specify "every *n*th time" with the suffix /*n*; for instance, both */12 and 0-59/12 mean 0,12,24,36,48 (i.e., every 12 minutes).

Hours of the day

Same syntax as for minutes.

Days of the month

Integers between 1 and 31; again, you may use sequences, ranges, sequences of ranges, or an asterisk.

Months of the year

    Integers between 1 and 12; again, you may use sequences, ranges, sequences of ranges, or an asterisk. Additionally, you may use three-letter abbreviations (jan, feb, mar, ...), but not in ranges or sequences.

Days of the week

    Integers between 0 (Sunday) and 6 (Saturday); again, you may use sequences, ranges, sequences of ranges, or an asterisk. Additionally, you may use three-letter abbreviations (sun, mon, tue, ...), but not in ranges or sequences.

Command to execute

    Any shell command, which will be executed in your login environment, so you can refer to environment variables like $HOME and expect them to work. Use only absolute paths to your commands (e.g., */usr/bin/who* instead of who) to ensure that cron is running the right programs, as a Linux system may have several programs with the same name.

Here are some example time specifications:

*	*	*	*	*	Every minute
45	*	*	*	*	45 minutes after each hour (1:45, 2:45, etc.)
45	9	*	*	*	Every day at 9:45 am
45	9	8	*	*	The eighth day of every month at 9:45 am
45	9	8	12	*	Every December 8 at 9:45 am
45	9	8	dec	*	Every December 8 at 9:45 am
45	9	*	*	6	Every Saturday at 9:45 am
45	9	*	*	sat	Every Saturday at 9:45 am
45	9	*	12	6	Every Saturday in December, at 9:45 am

| 45 | 9 | 8 | 12 | 6 | Every Saturday in December, plus December 8, at 9:45 am |

If the command produces any output upon execution, `cron` will email it to you (or more precisely, to the owning user for that crontab file: see the manpage for `cron`).

Logins, Logouts, and Shutdowns

We assume you know how to log into your Linux account. To log out using GNOME or KDE, choose Logout from the main menu. To log out from a remote shell, just close the shell (type `exit` or `logout`).

Never simply turn off the power to a Linux system: it needs a more graceful shutdown. To perform a shutdown from GNOME or KDE, use the main menu. To perform a shutdown from a shell, run the `shutdown` or `systemctl` command as the superuser, as follows.

---

shutdown   stdin **stdout** - file -- opt --help --version

```
shutdown [options] time [message]
```

The `shutdown` command halts or reboots a Linux system; only the superuser may run it. Here's a command to halt the system in 10 minutes, broadcasting the message "scheduled maintenance" to all users logged in:

→ **sudo shutdown -h +10 "scheduled maintenance"**

The *time* may be a number of minutes preceded by a plus sign, like +10; an absolute time in hours and minutes, like 16:25; or the word now to mean immediately.

With no options, `shutdown` puts the system into single-user mode, a special maintenance mode in which only one person is logged in (at the system console), and all nonessential services are off. To exit single-user mode, either perform another shut down to halt or reboot, or type ^D to bring up the system in normal, multiuser mode.

Useful options

- r   Reboot the system.

- h   Halt the system.

- k   Kidding: don't really perform a shutdown, just broadcast warning messages to all users as if the system were going down.

- c   Cancel a shutdown in progress (omit the *time* argument).

- f   On reboot, skip the usual filesystem check performed by the fsck program (described in "Disks and Filesystems" on page 131).

- F   On reboot, require the usual filesystem check.

For technical information about shutdowns, single-user mode, and various system states, see the manpages for init and init tab.

---

systemctl   **stdin**   **stdout** - file -- opt **--help** **--version**

```
systemctl [options] command [arguments]
```

In some Linux distros, the shutdown command is a symbolic link to systemctl, a multipurpose command for starting and stopping services, including the entire host. systemctl is part of a service manager called systemd; a full treatment is beyond the scope of this book, but we'll cover a few basic uses. (See *man systemd* for more details.)

```
sudo systemctl poweroff   Shut down the system.
sudo systemctl reboot     Reboot the system.
sudo systemctl suspend    Suspend the system.
```

Users and Their Environment

logname	Print your login name.
whoami	Print your current, effective username.
id	Print the user ID and group membership of a user.
who	List logged-in users, long output.
users	List logged-in users, short output.
finger	Print information about users.
last	Determine when someone last logged in.
printenv	Print your environment.

Who are you? Only the system knows for sure. This grab-bag of programs tells you all about *users*: their names, login times, and properties of their environment.

---

logname   stdin   **stdout**   - file   -- opt   **--help**   **--version**

logname

The logname command prints your login name (it might seem trivial, but it's useful in shell scripts):

→ **logname**
smith

If this command does not work on your system, try instead:

→ **echo $LOGNAME**

| **whoami** | stdin | **stdout** | - file | -- opt | **--help** | **--version** |

```
whoami
```

The whoami command prints the name of the current, effective user. This may differ from your login name (the output of logname) if you've used the sudo command. This example distinguishes whoami from logname:

```
→ logname
smith
→ sudo logname
smith
→ whoami
smith
→ sudo whoami
root
```

| **id** | stdin | **stdout** | - file | -- opt | **--help** | **--version** |

```
id [options] [username]
```

Every user has a unique, numeric *user ID*, and a default group with a unique, numeric *group ID*. The id command prints these values along with their associated user and group names:

```
→ id
uid=500(smith) gid=500(smith)
groups=500(smith),6(disk),490(src),501(cdwrite)
```

Useful options

- -u Print the effective user ID and exit.

- -g Print the effective group ID and exit.

- -G Print the IDs of all other groups to which the user belongs.

- `-n` Print names (for users and groups) rather than numeric IDs. Must be combined with `-u`, `-g`, or `-G`. For example, `id -Gn` produces the same output as the `groups` command.

- `-r` Print login values instead of effective values. Must be combined with `-u`, `-g`, or `-G`.

---

who

stdin   **stdout**   `-file`   `--opt`   **--help**   **--version**

who [*options*] [*filename*]

The who command lists all logged-in users, one user shell per line:

```
→ who
smith    pts/0    Sep  6 17:09 (:0)
barrett  pts/1    Sep  6 17:10 (10.24.19.240)
jones    pts/2    Sep  8 20:58 (192.168.13.7)
jones    pts/4    Sep  3 05:11 (192.168.13.7)
```

Normally, who gets its data from the file */var/run/utmp*. The *filename* argument can specify a different data file, such as */var/log/wtmp* for past logins or */var/log/btmp* for failed logins.[19]

Useful options

`-H`	Print a row of headings as the first line.
`--lookup`	For remotely logged-in users, print the hostnames of origin.
`-u`	Also print each user's idle time at his/her terminal.

---

19 If your system is configured to log this information.

-T	Also indicate whether each user's terminal is writable (see mesg in "Instant Messaging" on page 198). A plus sign means "yes," a minus sign means "no," and a question mark means "unknown."
-m	Display information only about yourself (i.e., the user associated with the current terminal).
-q	Quick display of usernames only, and a count of users. Much like the users command, but it adds a count.

users   stdin **stdout** - file -- opt **--help** **--version**

```
users [filename]
```

The users command prints a quick listing of users who have login sessions (if a user is running multiple shells, she appears multiple times):

```
→ users
barrett jones smith smith smith
```

Like the who command, users reads */var/log/utmp* by default but can read from another supplied file instead.

finger   stdin **stdout** - file -- opt **--help** **--version**

```
finger [options] [user[@host]]
```

The finger command prints logged-in user information in a short form:

```
→ finger
Login     Name              Tty     Idle  Login Time
smith     Sandy Smith       :0            Sep  6 17:09
barrett   Daniel Barrett    :pts/1  24    Sep  6 17:10
jones     Jill Jones        :pts/2        Sep  8 20:58
```

or a long form:

```
→ finger smith
Login: smith                           Name: Sandy Smith
Directory: /home/smith                 Shell: /bin/bash
On since Sat Sep  6 17:09 (EDT) on :0
Last login Mon Sep  8 21:07 (EDT) on pts/6 from web1
No mail.
Project:
Enhance world peace
Plan:
Mistrust first impulses; they are always right.
```

The *user* argument can be a local username or a remote user in the form *user@host*. Remote hosts will respond to finger requests only if they are configured to do so.

Useful options

- -l   Print in long format.

- -s   Print in short format.

- -p   Don't display the Project and Plan sections, which are ordinarily read from the user's ~/.project and ~/.plan files, respectively.

---

last   stdin   **stdout**   - file   **-- opt**   --help   --version

```
last [options] [users] [ttys]
```

The last command displays a history of logins, in reverse chronological order:

```
→ last
bob pts/3 localhost Mon Sep 8 21:07 - 21:08 (00:01)
sue pts/6 :0        Mon Sep 8 20:25 - 20:56 (00:31)
bob pts/4 myhost    Sun Sep 7 22:19 still logged in
...
```

You may provide usernames or tty names to limit the output.

Useful options

`-N`	Print only the latest *N* lines of output, where *N* is a positive integer.
`-i`	Display IP addresses instead of hostnames.
`-R`	Don't display hostnames.
`-x`	Also display system shutdowns and changes in system runlevel (e.g., from single-user mode into multiuser mode).
`-f filename`	Read from some other data file than */var/run/wtmp*; see the who command for more details.

---

printenv

```
printenv [environment_variables]
```

The printenv command prints all environment variables known to your shell and their values:

```
→ printenv
HOME=/home/smith
MAIL=/var/spool/mail/smith
NAME=Sandy Smith
SHELL=/bin/bash
...
```

or only specified variables:

```
→ printenv HOME SHELL
/home/smith
/bin/bash
```

User Account Management

`useradd`	Create an account.
`userdel`	Delete an account.

usermod	Modify an account.
passwd	Change a password.
chfn	Change a user's personal information.
chsh	Change a user's shell.

The installation process for your Linux distro undoubtedly prompted you to create a superuser account (root), and possibly also an ordinary user account (presumably for yourself). But you might want to create other accounts, too.

Creating users is an important job not to be taken lightly. Every account is a potential avenue for an intruder to enter your system, so every user should have a strong, hard-to-guess password.

---

useradd   stdin   **stdout**   - file   **-- opt**   --help   --version

useradd [*options*] *username*

The useradd command lets the superuser create a user account:

→ **sudo useradd smith**

Its defaults are not very useful (run useradd -D to see them), so be sure to supply all desired options. For example:

→ **sudo useradd -d /home/smith -s /bin/bash \
  -g users smith**

Useful options

-d *dir*	Set the user's home directory to be *dir*.
-s *shell*	Set the user's login shell to be *shell*.
-u *uid*	Set the user's ID to be *uid*. Unless you know what you're doing, omit this option and accept the default.

`-c string`	Set the user's comment field (historically called the GECOS field). This is usually the user's full name, but it can be any string. The `chfn` command can also set this information.
`-g group`	Set the user's initial (default) group to `group`, which can either be a numeric group ID or a group name, and which must already exist.
`-G group1,group2,...`	Make the user a member of the additional, existing groups `group1`, `group2`, and so on.
`-m`	Copy all files from your system skeleton directory, */etc/skel*, into the newly created home directory. The skeleton directory traditionally contains minimal (skeletal) versions of initialization files, like *~/.bash_profile*, to get new users started. If you prefer to copy from a different directory, add the `-k` option (`-k dirname`).

---

userdel

stdin   **stdout**   -file   **--opt**   --help   --version

userdel [-r] username

The userdel command deletes an existing user.

→ **sudo userdel smith**

It does not delete the files in the user's home directory unless you supply the -r option. Think carefully before deleting a user; consider deactivating the account instead (with usermod -L). And make sure you have backups of all the user's files before deleting them: you might need them again someday.

usermod

usermod [*options*] *username*

The usermod command modifies the given user's account in various ways, such as changing a home directory:

→ **sudo usermod -d /home/another smith**

Useful options

-d *dir*	Change the user's home directory to *dir*.
-l *username*	Change the user's login name to *username*. Think carefully before doing this, in case anything on your system depends on the original name. And don't change system accounts (root, daemon, etc.) unless you really know what you're doing!
-s *shell*	Change the user's login shell to *shell*.
-g *group*	Change the user's initial (default) group to *group*, which can either be a numeric group ID or a group name, and which must already exist.
-G *group1*, *group2*, ...	Make the user a member *only* of the additional, existing groups *group1*, *group2*, and so on. If the user previously belonged to other groups, but you don't specify them here, the user will no longer belong to them.
-L	Disable (lock) the account so the user cannot log in.
-U	Unlock the account after a lock (-L) operation.

passwd

passwd [*options*] [*username*]

The passwd command changes a login password, yours by default:

→ **passwd**

or another user's password if run by the superuser:

→ **sudo passwd smith**

passwd does have options, most of them related to password expiration. Use them only in the context of a well-thought-out security policy.

---

chfn

chfn [*options*] [*username*]

The chfn (change finger) command updates a few pieces of personal information maintained by the system: real name, home telephone, office telephone, and office location, as displayed by the finger command. Invoked without a username, chfn affects your account; invoked with a username (by root), it affects that user. With no options, chfn will prompt you for the desired information:

```
→ chfn
Password: ********
Name [Shawn Smith]: Shawn E. Smith
Office [100 Barton Hall]:
Office Phone [212-555-1212]: 212-555-1234
Home Phone []:
```

Useful options

-f *name*   Change the full name to *name*.

-h *phone*   Change the home phone number to *phone*.

-p *phone*   Change the office phone number to *phone*.

-o *office* Change the office location to *office*.

---

chsh   stdin   stdout   -file   --opt   --help   --version

chsh [*options*] [*username*]

The chsh (change shell) command sets your login shell program. Invoked without a username, chsh affects your account; invoked with a username (by root), it affects that user. With no options, chsh will prompt you for the desired information:

```
→ chsh
Changing shell for smith.
Password: *******
New shell [/bin/bash]: /bin/tcsh
```

The new shell must be listed in the file */etc/shells*.

Useful options

-s *shell*   Specify the new shell.

-l   List all permissible shells.

Becoming the Superuser

Normal users, for the most part, can modify only the files they own. One special user, called the *superuser* or *root*, has full access to the machine and can do anything on it. You should rarely need superuser privileges; and in fact, you should use them only when absolutely necessary, to avoid accidentally harming your Linux system.

You can become the superuser in several ways. One is to use the sudo command to gain superuser abilities for the duration of a single command. Simply type "sudo" followed by the command. You may be prompted for your password, depending on how sudo is configured on your machine:

```
→ sudo rm protected_file
Password: ********          Your own password
```

To make your superuser powers last for multiple commands, you can run a shell with sudo:

```
→ sudo bash
```

This is convenient, say, before browsing through many protected directories with cd. When finished executing commands as the superuser, type ^D or run exit to end the superuser shell and become yourself again. If you forget whether your shell is a superuser shell or just a normal one, check your identity with the whoami command. If you're the superuser, it will display root.

Another way to become the superuser is the su command, which also creates a superuser shell, but you'll need a different password, called the root password, to use it. If you don't know the root password on the system, you can't use su. (If you installed Linux yourself, you chose the root password during installation):

```
→ su -l
Password: *******          root password
#
```

Your shell prompt may change, often to a hash mark (#), to indicate you are the superuser.

If you provide a username to su:

```
→ su -l sophia
Password: *******          sophia's password
```

you can become that user (provided you know her password).

sudo and su have important differences. su is standard on every Linux system, but you need a password other than your own in order to run it. sudo uses your own password, but it must be configured to do so. sudo is superior for systems with multiple superusers, as it provides precise control over privileges (in the */etc/sudoers* file) and even logs the commands that get run. A full discussion is beyond the scope of this book: see man sudo and *http://www.sudo.ws/* for full details.

Group Management

groups   Print the group membership of a user.

groupadd   Create a group.

groupdel   Delete a group.

groupmod   Modify a group.

A *group* is a set of accounts treated as a single entity. If you give permission for a group to take some action (such as modify a file), then all members of that group can take it. For example, you can give full permissions for the group friends to read, write, and execute the file */tmp/sample*:

```
→ groups
users smith friends
→ chgrp friends /tmp/sample
→ chmod 770 /tmp/sample
→ ls -l /tmp/sample
-rwxrwx--- 1 smith friends 2874 … /tmp/sample
```

To add users to a group, edit */etc/group* as root.[20] To change the group ownership of a file, recall the chgrp commands from "File Properties" on page 69.

---

20 Different systems may store the group member list in other ways.

groups
stdin **stdout** - file -- opt **--help** **--version**

```
groups [usernames]
```

The groups command prints the Linux groups to which you belong, or to which other users belong:

```
→ whoami
smith
→ groups
smith users
→ groups jones root
jones : jones users
root : root bin daemon sys adm disk wheel src
```

---

groupadd
stdin stdout - file **-- opt** --help --version

```
groupadd [options] group
```

The groupadd command creates a group. In most cases, you should use the -f option to prevent duplicate groups from being created:

```
→ sudo groupadd -f friends
```

Useful options

-g *gid* Specify your own numeric group ID instead of letting groupadd choose one.

-f If the specified group exists already, complain and exit.

groupdel

stdin   stdout   - file   **-- opt**   --help   --version

groupdel *group*

The groupdel command deletes an existing group:

→ **sudo groupdel friends**

Before doing this, it's a good idea to identify all files that have their group ID set to the given group, so you can deal with them later:

→ **sudo find / -group friends -print**

because groupdel does not change the group ownership of any files. It simply removes the group name from the system's records. If you list such files, you'll see a numeric group ID in place of a group name.

---

groupmod

stdin   **stdout**   - file   **-- opt**   --help   --version

groupmod [*options*] *group*

The groupmod command modifies the given group, changing its name or group ID:

→ **sudo groupmod -n newname friends**

groupmod does not affect any files owned by this group: it simply changes the ID or name in the system's records. Be careful when changing the ID, or these files will have group ownership by a nonexistent group.

Useful options

-n *name*   Change the group's name to *name* (safe).

-g *gid*   Change the group's ID to *gid* (risky).

Host Information

uname	Print basic system information.
hostname	Print the system's hostname.
domainname	Same as hostname -y.
ip	Set and display network interface information.
ifconfig	Older command to set and display network interface information.

Every Linux machine (or *host*) has a name, a network IP address, and other properties. Here's how to display this information.

---

uname   stdin   **stdout**   - file   -- opt   --help   --version

uname [*options*]

The uname command prints fundamental information about your computer:

```
→ uname -a
Linux server.example.com 4.2.0-17-generic
  #21-Ubuntu SMP Fri Oct 23 19:56:16
  UTC 2015 x86_64 ... GNU/Linux
```

This includes the kernel name (Linux), hostname (server.example.com), kernel release (4.2.0-17-generic), kernel version (#21-Ubuntu SMP Fri Oct 23 19:56:16 UTC 2015), hardware name (x86_64), and operating system name (GNU/Linux). Each of these values can be printed individually using options.

Useful options

-a   All information.

-s Only the kernel name (the default).

-n Only the hostname, as with the hostname command.

-r Only the kernel release.

-v Only the kernel version.

-m Only the hardware name.

-p Only the processor type.

-i Only the hardware platform.

-o Only the operating system name.

---

hostname   stdin   stdout   - file   -- opt   --help   --version

hostname [*options*] [*name*]

The hostname command prints the name of your computer.
Depending on how you have things set up, this might be the
fully qualified hostname:

→ **hostname**
myhost.example.com

or your short hostname:

→ **hostname**
myhost

You can also set your hostname, as root:[21]

→ **sudo hostname orange**

---

21 This change might not survive a reboot. Some Linux distros require
    additional steps, such as placing the hostname into a configuration file
    that is read at boot time. Consult the documentation for your distro.

However, hostnames and nameservers are complicated topics well beyond the scope of this book. Don't just blindly start setting hostnames!

Useful options

-i	Print your host's IP address.
-a	Print your host's alias name.
-s	Print your host's short name.
-f	Print your host's fully qualified name.
-d	Print your host's DNS domain name.
-y	Print your host's NIS or YP domain name.
-F hostfile	Set your hostname by reading the name from file hostfile.

---

ip   stdin **stdout** - file -- opt **--help** --version

ip [options] object command...

The ip command displays and sets various aspects of your computer's network interface. This topic is beyond the scope of the book, but we'll teach you a few tricks.

You can get information about the default network interface (usually called *eth0*):

```
→ ip addr show eth0
2: eth0: <BROADCAST,MULTICAST,UP,LOWER_UP>...
   link/ether 00:50:ba:48:4f:ba brd ff:ff:ff:...
   inet 192.168.0.21/24 brd 192.168.0.255 scope ...
   inet6 fe80::21e:8cff:fe53:41e4/64 ...
```

This includes your MAC address (00:50:ba:48:4f:ba), your IP address (192.168.0.21), and various other information. To view all loaded network interfaces, run:

→ `ip addr show`

Some other useful commands for displaying network information include:

`ip help`
> See usage information for all these commands.

`ip addr`
> Display IP addresses of your network devices.

`ip maddr`
> Display multicast addresses of your network devices.

`ip link`
> Display attributes of your network devices.

`ip route`
> Display your routing table.

`ip monitor`
> Begin monitoring your network devices; type ^C to stop.

Each of these commands has various options: add `help` on the end (e.g., `ip link help`) for usage. Additionally, `ip` can modify your network when run by the superuser: configuring your network devices, managing routing tables and rules, creating tunnels, and more. It's part of a suite of tools called *iproute2*. You'll need networking experience to understand this complex command; see the `ip` manpage to get started, or visit *http://lartc.org*.

---

ifconfig   stdin   **stdout**   - file   -- opt   **--help**   **--version**

`ifconfig [options] interface`

The `ifconfig` command is an ancestor of `ip`. It is still found on many Linux systems but is less powerful (some would call it obsolete). We'll cover a few simple commands here, but you should be using `ip` instead.

To display information about the default network interface (usually called *eth0*):

```
→ ifconfig eth0
eth0  Link encap:Ethernet  HWaddr 00:50:BA:48:4F:BA
  inet addr:192.168.0.21  Bcast:192.168.0.255 …
  UP BROADCAST RUNNING MULTICAST  MTU:1500 …
  RX packets:1955231 errors:0 dropped:0 overruns:0 …
  TX packets:1314765 errors:0 dropped:0 overruns:0 …
  collisions:0 txqueuelen:100
  …
```

This includes your MAC address (00:50:BA:48:4F:BA), your IP address (192.168.0.21), your netmask (255.255.255.0), and various other information. To view all loaded network interfaces, run:

```
→ ifconfig -a
```

Host Location

host	Look up hostnames, IP addresses, and DNS info.
whois	Look up the registrants of Internet domains.
ping	Check if a remote host is reachable.
traceroute	View the network path to a remote host.

When dealing with remote computers, you might want to know more about them. Who owns them? What are the IP addresses? Where on the network are they located?

---

host   stdin   **stdout**   - file   **-- opt**   --help   --version

host [*options*] *name* [*server*]

The host command looks up the hostname or IP address of a remote machine by querying DNS:

```
→ host www.ubuntu.org
www.ubuntu.com has address 91.189.90.41
→ host 91.189.90.41
41.90.189.91.in-addr.arpa domain name pointer
 jujube.canonical.com.
```

It can also find out much more:

```
→ host -a www.ubuntu.org
Trying "www.ubuntu.org"
;; ->>HEADER<<- opcode: QUERY, status: NOERROR ...
;; flags: qr rd ra; QUERY: 1, ANSWER: 1, ...

;; QUESTION SECTION:
;www.ubuntu.org.                        IN      ANY

;; ANSWER SECTION:
www.ubuntu.org.      60      IN      CNAME
ubuntu.org.
```

though a full discussion of this output is beyond the scope of this book. The final, optional "server" parameter specifies a particular nameserver for the query:

```
→ host www.ubuntu.org ns2.dondominio.com
Using domain server:
Name: ns2.dondominio.com
Address: 93.93.67.2#53
Aliases:

www.ubuntu.org is an alias for ubuntu.org.
ubuntu.org has address 147.83.195.55
ubuntu.org mail is handled by 10 mx2.upc.es.
ubuntu.org mail is handled by 10 mx1.upc.es.
```

To see all options, type host by itself.

Useful options

-a Display all available information.

> -t Choose the type of nameserver query: A, AXFR, CNAME, HINFO, KEY, MX, NS, PTR, SIG, SOA, and so on.

Here's an example of the -t option to locate MX records:

```
→ host -t MX redhat.com
redhat.com mail is handled by 5 mx1.redhat.com.
redhat.com mail is handled by 10 mx2.redhat.com.
```

If the host command doesn't do what you want, try dig, another powerful DNS lookup utility. You might also encounter the nslookup command, mostly obsolete but still found on some Linux and Unix systems.

---

whois   stdin **stdout** - file -- **opt** --**help** --**version**

whois [*options*] *domain_name*

The whois command looks up the registration of an Internet domain:

```
→ whois linuxmint.com
...
Domain name: LINUXMINT.COM
Registrar: TUCOWS DOMAINS INC.
...
 Administrative Contact:
    Lefebvre, Clement
...
 Technical Contact:
    Hostmaster, Servage
...
Creation Date: 07-jun-2006
Expiration Date: 07-jun-2016
...
```

plus a few screens full of legal disclaimers from the registrar.

Useful options

-h *registrar*   Perform the lookup at the given registrar's server. For
                        example, whois -h whois.networksolutions.com
                        yahoo.com.

-p *port*   Query the given TCP port instead of the default, 43 (the
                        whois service).

---

ping
                        stdin   **stdout**   - file   **-- opt**   --help   --version

ping [*options*] *host*

The ping command tells you if a remote host is reachable. It
sends small packets (ICMP packets to be precise) to a remote
host and waits for responses:

```
→ ping google.com
PING google.com (74.125.226.144) from 192.168.0.10 :
56(84) bytes of data.
64 bytes from www.google.com (74.125.226.144):
  icmp_seq=0 ttl=49 time=32.390 msec
64 bytes from www.google.com (74.125.226.144):
  icmp_seq=1 ttl=49 time=24.208 msec
^C
--- google.com ping statistics ---
2 packets transmitted, 2 packets received,
 0% packet loss
round-trip min/avg/max/mdev =
 24.208/28.299/32.390/4.091 ms
```

Useful options

-c *N*   Ping at most *N* times.

-i *N*   Wait *N* seconds (default 1) between pings.

-n   Print IP addresses in the output, rather than hostnames.

---

traceroute

stdin   **stdout**   - file   **-- opt**   **--help**   **--version**

traceroute [*options*] *host* [*packet_length*]

The traceroute command prints the network path from your local host to a remote host, and the time it takes for packets to traverse the path:

```
→ traceroute yahoo.com
  1 server.mydomain.com (192.168.0.20) 1.397 ms ...
  2 10.221.16.1 (10.221.16.1) 15.397 ms ...
  3 router.example.com (92.242.140.21) 4.952 ms ...
 ...
 ...
 16 p6.www.dcn.yahoo.com (216.109.118.69)  * ...
```

Each host in the path is sent three "probes" and the return times are reported. If five seconds pass with no response, traceroute prints an asterisk. Also, traceroute may be blocked by firewalls or unable to proceed for various reasons, in which case it prints a symbol:

Symbol	Meaning
!F	Fragmentation needed.
!H	Host unreachable.
!N	Network unreachable.
!P	Protocol unreachable.
!S	Source route failed.
!X	Communication administratively prohibited.
!*N*	ICMP unreachable code *N*.

The default packet size is 40 bytes, but you can change this with the final, optional *packet_length* parameter (e.g., traceroute myhost 120).

Host Location | 183

Useful options

-n Numeric mode: print IP addresses instead of hostnames.

-w *N* Change the timeout from five seconds to *N* seconds.

Network Connections

ssh Securely log into a remote host, or run commands on it.

scp Securely copy files to/from a remote host (batch).

sftp Securely copy files to/from a remote host (interactive).

ftp   Copy files to/from a remote host (interactive, insecure!).

netcat Create arbitrary network connections.

With Linux, it's easy to establish network connections from one machine to another for remote logins and file transfers. Just make sure you do it securely.

---

ssh   **stdin stdout** - file -- opt --help --version

ssh [*options*] *host* [*command*]

The ssh (Secure Shell) program securely logs you into a remote machine where you already have an account:

→ **ssh remote.example.com**

Alternatively, it can invoke a program on that remote machine without logging you in:

→ **ssh remote.example.com who**

ssh encrypts all data that travels across its connection, including your username and password (which you'll need to access the remote machine). The SSH protocol also supports other ways to authenticate, such as public keys and host IDs. See man sshd for details.

Useful options

- `-l user`   Specify your remote username; otherwise, ssh assumes your local username. You can also use the syntax *username@host*:
    → `ssh smith@server.example.com`

- `-p port`   Use a *port* number other than the default (22).

- `-t`   Allocate a tty on the remote system; useful when trying to run a remote command with an interactive user interface, such as a text editor.

- `-v`   Produce verbose output, useful for debugging.

---

scp   stdin   **stdout**   - file   -- opt   **--help**   **--version**

`scp` *local_spec remote_spec*

The scp (secure copy) command copies files and directories from one computer to another in batch. (For an interactive user interface, see sftp.) It encrypts all communication between the two machines. As a simple example, scp can copy a local file to a remote machine:

→ `scp myfile remote.example.com:newfile`

recursively copy a directory to a remote machine:

→ `scp -r mydir remote.example.com:`

copy a remote file to your local machine:

→ `scp remote.example.com:myfile .`

or recursively copy a remote directory to your local machine:

→ `scp -r remote.example.com:mydir .`

To specify an alternate username on the remote system, use the *username@host* syntax:

→ `scp myfile smith@remote.example.com:`

Useful options

-p Duplicate all file attributes (permissions, timestamps) when copying.

-r Recursively copy a directory and its contents.

-v Produce verbose output, useful for debugging.

---

sftp	stdin	stdout	- file	-- opt	--help	--version

```
sftp (host username@host)
```

The sftp program copies files interactively and securely between two computers. (As opposed to scp, which copies files in batch.) The user interface is much like that of ftp, but ftp is not secure:

```
→ sftp remote.example.com
Password: ********
sftp> cd MyFiles
sftp> ls
README
file1
file2
file3
sftp> get file2
Fetching /home/smith/MyFiles/file2 to file2
sftp> quit
```

If your username on the remote system is different from your local one, use the *username@host* argument:

```
→ sftp smith@remote.example.com
```

Command	Meaning
help	View a list of available commands.
ls	List the files in the current remote directory.
lls	List the files in the current local directory.

Command	Meaning
pwd	Print the remote working directory.
lpwd	Print the local working directory.
cd *dir*	Change your remote directory to be *dir*.
lcd *dir*	Change your local directory to be *dir*.
get *file1* [*file2*]	Copy remote *file1* to local machine, optionally renamed as *file2*.
put *file1* [*file2*]	Copy local *file1* to remote machine, optionally renamed as *file2*.
mget *file**	Copy multiple remote files to the local machine using wildcards * and ?.
mput *file**	Copy multiple local files to the remote machine using wildcards * and ?.
quit	Exit sftp.

ftp   stdin   stdout   - file   -- opt   --help   --version

ftp [*options*] *host*

The popular ftp (File Transfer Protocol) program copies files between computers, but not in a secure manner: your username and password travel over the network as plain text. Use sftp instead if your remote server supports it.

The same commands we listed for sftp also work for ftp. (However, the two programs support other, differing commands, too.)

```
netcat [options] [destination] [port]

nc [options] [destination] [port]
```

netcat, or equivalently, nc, is a general-purpose tool for making
network connections. It's handy for debugging, learning about
networking, and many other uses. For example, netcat can
speak directly to any TCP or UDP service, such as an SSH
server on your local TCP port 22:

```
→ netcat localhost 22
SSH-2.0-OpenSSH_6.9p1 Ubuntu-2ubuntu0.1
^C
```

This feature, which is handy for determining if a particular service is up or down, also works with service names as listed
in */etc/services*. For example, you could connect to Google's web
service (port 80) with:

```
→ netcat www.google.com http
xxx                          Type some junk and press Enter
HTTP/1.0 400 Bad Request
Content-Type: text/html; charset=UTF-8
Content-Length: 1555
Date: Fri, 04 Mar 2016 02:17:37 GMT
...
```

If you're an old-school Linux user, you might be using telnet
for connecting in this way to arbitrary TCP ports. netcat is
much more flexible. For example, using two shells, you can create a client and a service and have them talk to each other. Start
a service listening on port 55555:

```
→ netcat -l 55555
```

Now in another window, run a client that talks to that same
port, and type a message:

```
→ netcat localhost 55555
Hello world, how are you?
```

Your message gets sent to your service, which will print "Hello world, how are you?" and any subsequent lines you enter. Press ^D to close the connection.

Useful options

-u   Establish a UDP connection instead of TCP.

-l   Listen for connections on the given port.

-p *N*   Use port *N* as the source port.

-w *N*   Time out after *N* seconds.

-h   Get help.

Email

mutt   Text-based mail client.

mail   Minimal text-based mail client.

mailq   View the outgoing mail queue on your system.

Linux includes a number of text-based mail clients. We'll look at several with different purposes and strengths. (Linux also has graphical email clients, such as Thunderbird, Evolution, and KMail.)

---

mutt   **stdin**   **stdout**   - file   -- opt   --help   --version

mutt [*options*]

Mutt is a text-based mailer that runs in an ordinary terminal (or terminal window), so it can be used both locally (e.g., in an X terminal window) or remotely over an SSH connection. It is very powerful, with many commands and options. To invoke it, type:

   → mutt

When the main screen appears, any messages in your mailbox are listed briefly, one per line, and the following commands are available:

Keystroke	Meaning
Up arrow	Move to the previous message.
Down arrow	Move to the next message.
PageUp	Scroll up one pageful of messages.
PageDown	Scroll down one pageful of messages.
Home	Move to the first message.
End	Move to the last message.
m	Compose a new mail message. This invokes your default text editor. After editing the message and exiting the editor, type y to send the message or q to postpone it.
r	Reply to current message. Works like m.
f	Forward the current message to a third party. Works like m.
i	View the contents of your mailbox.
C	Copy the current message to another mailbox.
d	Delete the current message.

While writing a message, after you exit your text editor, the following commands are available:

Keystroke	Meaning
a	Attach a file (an attachment) to the message.
c	Set the CC list.
b	Set the BCC list.
e	Edit the message again.
r	Edit the Reply-To field.
s	Edit the subject line.
y	Send the message.

Keystroke	Meaning
C	Copy the message to a file.
q	Postpone the message without sending it.

Additional commands are always available:

Keystroke	Meaning
?	See a list of all commands (press the SPACEBAR to scroll down, q to quit).
^G	Cancel the command in progress.
q	Quit.

The official Mutt site is *http://www.mutt.org*. For a different command-line mail client for Linux, check out alpine (*http://patches.freeiz.com/*).

---

mail   **stdin** **stdout** - file -- opt --help --version

mail [*options*] *recipient*

The mail program is a quick, simple email client. Most people want a more powerful program for regular use, but for quick messages from the command line or in scripts, mail is really handy.

To send a quick message:

```
→ mail smith@example.com
Subject: my subject
I'm typing a message.
To end it, I type a period by itself on a line.
.
Cc: jones@example.com
→
```

To send a quick message using a single command, use a pipeline:

```
→ echo "Hey!" | mail -s "subject" smith@example.com
```

To mail a file using a single command, you can use redirection
or a pipeline:

```
→ mail -s "my subject" smith@example.com < filename
→ cat filename \
  | mail -s "my subject" smith@example.com
```

Notice how easily you can send the output of a pipeline as an
email message; this is useful in scripts.

Useful options

-s *subject*	Set the subject line of an outgoing message.
-v	Verbose mode: print messages about mail delivery.
-c *addresses*	CC the message to the given addresses, a comma-separated list.
-b *addresses*	BCC the message to the given addresses, a comma-separated list.

---

mailq   stdin   **stdout**   - file   -- opt   --help   --version

```
mailq
```

The mailq command lists any outgoing email messages await-
ing delivery, if any (mail delivery is usually so quick, however,
that mailq typically has no output):

```
→ mailq
...Size-- ----Arrival Time-- -Sender/Recipient---
    333 Tue Jan 10 21:17:14 smith@example.com
                            jones@elsewhere.org
```

Sent mail messages are also recorded in a log file such as */var/log/mail.log*; the name may differ from distro to distro. To see the most recent mail delivery actions, view the last few lines with `tail`:

→ `tail /var/log/mail.log`

Beyond Mail Readers

Email is more "transparent" on Linux than on other platforms that merely display your mailbox and send and receive messages. The ability to list outgoing email messages with `mailq` is just one example. Here are some other options to whet your appetite and encourage you to explore.

- You can process your mailboxes with any command-line tools, such as `grep`, because mail files are plain text.

- You can manually retrieve messages from your mail server at the command line with the `fetchmail` command. Using a simple configuration file, this command can reach out to IMAP and POP servers and download mail in batch. See `man fetchmail`.

- Your system can run a mail server, such as `postfix` or `sendmail`, to handle the most complex mail delivery situations.

- You can control local mail delivery in sophisticated ways with the `procmail` command, which filters arriving email messages through any arbitrary program. For more information, see `man procmail`.

- Spam filtering is sophisticated on Linux: check out the SpamAssassin suite of programs. You can run it personally on your incoming email, or at the server level for large numbers of users.

In short, email is not limited to the features of your mail-reading program. Investigate and experiment!

Web Browsing

lynx   Text-only web browser.

wget   Download web pages and files.

Besides the usual web browsers such as Chrome and Firefox, Linux offers several ways to explore the World Wide Web via the command line.

---

lynx   stdin   stdout   - file   -- opt   --help   --version

```
lynx [options] [URL]
```

Lynx is a stripped-down, text-only web browser. It doesn't display pictures, play audio or video, or even respond to your mouse. But it's incredibly useful when you just want a quick look at a page, or when the network is slow, or for downloading the HTML of a website. It's particularly good for checking out a suspicious URL, as Lynx doesn't run JavaScript and won't even accept a cookie without asking you first.

→ **lynx http://www.yahoo.com**

All browsing is done by keyboard. Many pages will not look quite right, especially if they use tables or frames extensively, but usually you can find your way around a site.

Keystroke	Meaning
?	Get help.
k	List all keystrokes and their meanings.
^G	Cancel a command in progress.
q	Quit Lynx.

Keystroke	Meaning
Enter	"Click" the current link, or finish the current form field.
Left arrow	Back to previous page.
Right arrow	Forward to next page, or "click" the current link.
g	Go to a URL (you'll be prompted to enter it).
p	Save, print, or mail the current page.
Space bar	Scroll down.
b	Scroll up.
Down arrow	Go to the next link or form field.
Up arrow	Go to the previous link or form field.
^A	Go to top of page.
^E	Go to end of page.
m	Return to the main/home page.
/	Search for text on the page.
a	Bookmark the current page.
v	View your bookmark list.
r	Delete a bookmark.
=	Display properties of the current page and link.
\	View HTML source (type again to return to normal view).

Lynx has over 100 command-line options, so the manpage is well worth exploring. If you like text-based browsing but Lynx isn't to your taste, try similar programs such as w3m, links, and elinks.

Useful options

-dump   Print the rendered page to standard output and exit.
                       (Compare to the -source option.)

`-source`	Print the HTML source to standard output and exit. (Compare to the wget command.)
`-emacskeys`	Make Lynx obey keystrokes reminiscent of the emacs editor.
`-vikeys`	Make Lynx obey keystrokes reminiscent of the vim (or vi) editor.
`-homepage=URL`	Set your home page URL to be *URL*.
`-color`	Turn colored text mode on.
`-nocolor`	Turn colored text mode off.

---

wget   stdin stdout - file -- opt --help --version

`wget [options] URL`

The wget command hits a URL and downloads the data to a file or standard output. It's great for capturing individual web pages, downloading files, or duplicating entire website hierarchies to arbitrary depth. For example, let's capture the Yahoo! home page:

```
→ wget http://www.yahoo.com
23:19:51 (220.84 KB/s) - 'index.html' saved [31434]
```

which is saved to a file *index.html* in the current directory. wget has the added ability to resume a download if it gets interrupted in the middle, say, due to a network failure: just run wget -c with the same URL and it picks up where it left off.

Perhaps the most useful feature of wget is its ability to download files without needing a web browser:

```
→ wget http://linuxpocketguide.com/sample.pdf
```

This is great for large files like videos and ISO images. You can even write shell scripts to download sets of files if you know their names:

```
→ for i in 1 2 3
do
  wget http://example.com/$i.mpeg
done
```

Another similar command is `curl`, which writes to standard output by default—unlike `wget`, which duplicates the original page and file names by default:

```
→ curl http://www.yahoo.com > mypage.html
```

`wget` has over 70 options, so we'll cover just a few important ones. (`curl` has a different set of options; see its manpage.)

Useful options

`-i filename`	Read URLs from the given file and retrieve them in turn.
`-O filename`	Write all the captured HTML to the given file, one page appended after the other.
`-c`	Continue mode: if a previous retrieval was interrupted, leaving only a partial file as a result, pick up where `wget` left off. That is, if `wget` had downloaded 100K of a 150K file, the `-c` option says to retrieve only the remaining 50K and append it to the existing file. `wget` can be fooled, however, if the remote file has changed since the first (partial) download, so use this option only if you know the remote file hasn't changed.
`-t N`	Try *N* times before giving up. *N*=0 means try forever.
`--progress=dot`	Print dots to show the download progress.
`--progress=bar`	Print bars to show the download progress.
`--spider`	Don't download, just check existence of remote pages.
`-nd`	Retrieve all files into the current directory, even if remotely they are in a more complex directory tree. (By default, `wget` duplicates the remote directory hierarchy.)
`-r`	Retrieve a page hierarchy recursively, including subdirectories.

-l *N*	Retrieve files at most *N* levels deep (5 by default).
-k	Inside retrieved files, modify URLs so the files can be viewed locally in a web browser.
-p	Download all necessary files to make a page display completely, such as stylesheets and images.
-L	Follow relative links (within a page) but not absolute links.
-A *pattern*	Accept mode: download only files whose names match a given pattern. Patterns may contain the same wildcards as the shell.
-R *pattern*	Reject mode: download only files whose names *do not* match a given pattern.
-I *pattern*	Directory inclusion: download files only from directories that match a given pattern.
-X *pattern*	Directory exclusion: download files only from directories that *do not* match a given pattern.

Instant Messaging

write	Send messages to a terminal.
mesg	Prohibit write.
tty	Print your terminal device name.
sendxmpp	Send instant messages via XMPP (Jabber).
profanity	Text-based XMPP client.
irssi	Text-based IRC client.

Linux provides two types of instant messaging. The first is for contacting other users on the same Linux machine, using an ancient command called write. The second is modern instant messaging, with commands such as sendxmpp. In the second case, it's more common to use a graphical instant messaging program such as pidgin (*http://www.pidgin.im/*), but command-line tools are helpful if you aren't using a graphical desktop.

write

```
write user [tty]
```

The write program sends lines of text from one logged-in user to another on the same Linux machine:

```
→ write smith
Hi, how are you?
See you later.
^D
```

^D ends the connection. write is also useful in pipelines for quick one-off messages:

```
→ echo 'Howdy!' | write smith
```

The related command wall sends a message to all logged-in users at once:

```
→ wall The system will reboot in 1 hour
```

mesg

```
mesg [y|n]
```

The mesg program controls whether write connections can reach your terminal. mesg y permits them, mesg n denies them, and mesg prints the current status (y or n); y is the default. mesg has no effect on modern instant messaging programs:

```
→ mesg
is y
→ mesg n
→ mesg
is n
```

tty   stdin   stdout   - file   -- opt   **--help**   **--version**

tty

The tty program prints the name of the terminal device associated with the current shell (write may need this information if your recipient is logged in multiple times):

→ **tty**
/dev/pts/4

---

sendxmpp   stdin   **stdout**   - file   -- opt   **--help**   **--version**

sendxmpp [*options*] recipients

The sendxmpp command provides a quick way to send an instant message via the XMPP protocol (Jabber). It's convenient when you just want to send a single message, which can be a simple "hello" or the contents of a text file, and you don't need to receive a message in return.

You'll need a Jabber username and password first, which you can obtain by registering on any Jabber server around the Web; visit *http://www.jabber.org* for a list of servers. Once you've registered, put your username and password into the file *~/.sendxmpp* in your home directory. Different versions of sendxmpp use different file formats. If your username is smith, your Jabber server is jabber.example.com, and your password is wQVY6LC/8pCH, the older file format is:

smith@jabber.example.com wQVY6LC/8pCH

and the newer format is:

username: smith
jserver: jabber.example.com
password: wQVY6LC/8pCH

Once this setup is complete, you can send a message to a friend on Jabber with:

```
→ echo "Hello world" | sendxmpp user@host
```

Many Jabber servers use secure connections, so you will probably need to add the option -t (for TLS connections) or -e (for SSL connections) for your command to work. Here's an example that secures the connection with TLS and sends the contents of a text file *message.txt* file:

```
→ sendxmpp -t user@host < message.txt
```

Useful options

-t	Use TLS to secure the connection.
-e	Use SSL to secure the connection.
-s *text*	Send a subject line along with your message.
-v	Verbose mode: print debugging information. Helpful if your connection fails.

---

profanity   stdin   stdout   - file   -- opt   **--help**   **--version**

profanity [*options*]

The profanity command is a fully functional instant messaging client for the XMPP protocol (Jabber). Unlike graphical clients, profanity runs in a shell window, so you can use it over SSH, for example.

You'll need a Jabber username and password, as with sendxmpp:

```
→ profanity -a user@host
```

profanity then prompts you for commands, which always begin with a slash. For example, to open a text-based "window" for messaging with a friend, enter:

```
/msg friend@jabber.example.com
```

and to send a message to that friend, enter:

```
/msg Hi there!
```

Selected commands

`/help`	Get help on all available commands.
`/connect` *you@host*	Log in.
`/msg` *user@host*	Open a messaging window to communicate with *user@host*.
`/msg` *text*	Send an instant message in your current messaging window.
`/close`	Close the current messaging window.
`/wins`	List your messaging windows.
F1–F10	Switch between messaging windows 1 through 10. (Does not work over SSH.)
`/disconnect`	Log out.
`/quit`	Exit profanity.

---

irssi stdin stdout - file -- opt **--help** **--version**

```
irssi [options]
```

The irssi command is a fully functional IRC (Internet Relay Chat) client that is text-based, so it runs in a shell window. A full tutorial on chatting with IRC is beyond the scope of this book: see *https://irssi.org* and *http://irchelp.org* for more information. To get started, run:

→ **irssi**

irssi then prompts you to type something. This can either be a command, which begins with a slash, or any other text, which

---

is broadcast as a message to everyone else connected to your current IRC channel:

```
→ irssi
[[status]] /connect irc.example.com
... Irssi: Connection to irc.example.com established
[[status]] /nick zippy
You're now known as zippy
[[status]] /join test
Irssi: Join to #test was synced in 0 secs
<zerbina> Hi there, zippy!
<fuelrod> Welcome back!
[#test] Are we having fun yet?
<zippy> Are we having fun yet?
<fuelrod> Totally!
<zerbina> Yow!
[#test] /quit
```

Selected commands

/help	List the available commands. For help on a single command, type /help /command. For example: /help /join
/connect server	Connect to an IRC server.
/nick name	Set your IRC nickname.
/join channel	Join a given IRC channel.
/names	List the users connected on the current channel.
/disconnect	Disconnect from the IRC server.
/quit	Exit irssi.

Screen Output

echo	Print simple text on standard output.
printf	Print formatted text on standard output.
yes	Print repeated text on standard output.

| seq | Print a sequence of numbers on standard output. |
| clear | Clear the screen or window. |

Linux provides several commands for printing messages on standard output, such as echo:

```
→ echo hello world
hello world
```

Each command has different strengths and intended purposes. These commands are invaluable for learning about Linux, debugging problems, writing shell scripts (see "Programming with Shell Scripts" on page 239), or just talking to yourself.

---

echo   stdin **stdout** - file -- opt --help --version

echo [*options*] *strings*

The echo command simply prints its arguments:

```
→ echo We are having fun
We are having fun
```

Confusingly, there are several different echo commands with slightly different behavior. There's */bin/echo*, but Linux shells typically override this with a built-in command called echo. To find out which you're using, run the command:

```
→ type echo
echo is a shell builtin
```

Useful options

- -n Don't print a final newline character.

- -e Recognize and interpret escape characters. For example, try echo 'hello \a' and echo -e 'hello\a'. The first prints literally and the second makes a beep.

- E   Don't interpret escape characters: the opposite of - e.

Available escape characters are:

\a	Alert (play a beep)
\b	Backspace
\c	Don't print the final newline (same effect as - n)
\f	Form feed
\n	Line feed (newline)
\r	Carriage return
\t	Horizontal tab
\v	Vertical tab
\\	A backslash
\'	Single quote
\"	Double quote
\nnn	The character whose ASCII value is nnn in octal

---

printf   stdin   **stdout**   - file   **-- opt**   --help   --version

printf *format_string* [*arguments*]

The printf command is an enhanced echo: it prints formatted strings on standard output. It operates much like the C programming language function printf(), which applies a format string to a sequence of arguments to create some specified output. For example:

→ **printf "User %s is %d years old.\n" sandy 29**
User sandy is 29 years old.

The first argument is the format string, which in our example contains two format specifications, %s and %d. The subsequent arguments, sandy and 29, are substituted by printf into the format string and then printed. Format specifications can get fancy with floating-point numbers:

```
→ printf "That\'ll be $%0.2f, sir.\n" 3
That'll be $3.00, sir.
```

There are two printf commands available in Linux: one built into the bash shell, and one in */usr/bin/printf*. The two are identical except for one format specification, %q, supported only by the bash built-in: it prints escape symbols ("\") so its output can be used as shell input safely. Note the difference:

```
→ printf "This is a quote: %s\n" "\""
This is a quote: "
→ printf "This is a quote: %q\n" "\""
This is a quote: \"
```

It is your responsibility to make sure the number of format specifications (%) equals the number of arguments supplied to printf. If you have too many arguments, the extras are ignored, and if you have too few, printf assumes default values (0 for numeric formats, an empty string for string formats). Nevertheless, you should treat such mismatches as errors, even though printf is forgiving. If they lurk in your shell scripts, they are bugs waiting to happen.

Format specifications are described in detail on the manpage for the C function printf (see man 3 printf). Here are some useful ones:

%d	Decimal integer
%ld	Long decimal integer
%o	Octal integer
%x	Hexadecimal integer
%f	Floating point
%lf	Double-precision floating point
%c	A single character

%s	String
%q	String with any shell metacharacters escaped
%%	A percent sign by itself

Just after the leading percent sign, you can insert a numeric expression for the minimum width of the output. For example, "%5d" means to print a decimal number in a five-character-wide field, and "%6.2f" means a floating-point number in a six-character-wide field with two digits after the decimal point. Some useful numeric expressions are:

n	Minimum width *n*.
0*n*	Minimum width *n*, padded with leading zeros.
n.m	Minimum width *n*, with *m* digits after the decimal point.

printf also interprets escape characters like "\n" (print a newline character) and "\a" (ring the bell). See the echo command for the full list.

---

yes

stdin   **stdout**   - file   -- opt   **--help**   **--version**

yes [*string*]

The yes command prints the given string (or "y" by default) forever, one string per line:

```
→ yes again
again
again
again
...
```

Though it might seem useless at first glance, yes can be perfect for turning interactive commands into batch commands. Want to get rid of an annoying "Are you SURE you want to do that?"

message? Pipe the output of yes into the input of the command to answer all those prompts:

```
→ yes | my_interactive_command
```

When my_interactive_command terminates, so will yes.

---

seq   stdin   **stdout**   - file   -- opt   **--help**   **--version**

```
seq [options] specification
```

The seq command prints a sequence of integers or real numbers, suitable for piping to other programs. There are three kinds of specification arguments:

A single number: an upper limit

   seq begins at 1 and counts up to the number:

```
→ seq 3
1
2
3
```

Two numbers: lower and upper limit

   seq begins at the first number and counts as far as it can without passing the second number:

```
→ seq 2 5
2
3
4
5
```

Three numbers: lower limit, increment, and upper limit

   seq begins at the first number, increments by the second number, and stops at (or before) the third number:

```
→ seq 1 .3 2
1
1.3
1.6
1.9
```

You can also go backward with a negative increment:

```
→ seq 5 -1 2
5
4
3
2
```

Useful options

-w   Print leading zeros, as necessary, to give all lines the same width:

```
→ seq -w 8 10
08
09
10
```

-f *format*   Format the output lines with a printf-like format string, which must include either %g (the default), %e, or %f:

```
→ seq -f '**%g**' 3
**1**
**2**
**3**
```

-s *string*   Use the given string as a separator between the numbers. By default, a newline is printed (i.e., one number per line):

```
→ seq -s ':' 10
1:2:3:4:5:6:7:8:9:10
```

---

clear   stdin   **stdout**   - file   -- opt   --help   --version

clear

This command simply clears your display or shell window.

Copy and Paste

xclip   Copy and paste between the shell and the clipboard.

---

xsel   Manipulate the clipboard from the shell.

Linux has a clipboard for copying and pasting between graphical applications. Actually, Linux has three different clipboards, which are called *selections*. You can access the selections from the command line, sending the output of any shell command to the selection, or reading the selection like standard input. Note that these commands work only if your shell is running in a graphical environment such as GNOME or KDE. Otherwise, no selection exists.

---

xclip
stdin   stdout   - file   -- opt   **-help   -version**

```
xclip [options]
```

xclip reads and writes the three Linux selections (clipboards), so you can copy and paste text between the shell and graphical applications. To see it in action, use your mouse to copy some text to a selection—say, double-click a word in your terminal window—and then run:

→ **xclip -o**

The text you copied will be printed on standard output. As another example, copy the contents of a file to a selection, and then print the selection:

```
→ cat poem                        See the file
Once upon a time, there was
a little operating system named
Linux, which everybody loved.
→ cat poem | xclip -i             Pipe file to selection
→ xclip -o                        Print selection
Once upon a time, there was
a little operating system named
Linux, which everybody loved.
```

All command-line options for xclip use single dashes, even
-help and -version.

Useful options

-selection *name*	Choose a selection by name, either primary, secondary, or clipboard. The default is primary. In my terminal windows, the mouse's middle button pastes from primary, but the right-button menu uses clipboard for its "Paste" command.
-i	Read the selection contents from standard input. You may omit this option.
-o	Write the selection contents to standard output.

---

xsel

stdin   stdout   - file   -- opt   --help   --version

xsel [*options*]

xsel is a more powerful version of xclip. Along with reading
and writing the three selections (clipboards), it can also append
to them, swap them, and clear them:

```
→ echo Hello | xsel -i
→ xsel -o
Hello
→ echo World | xsel -a        Append
→ xsel -o
Hello
World
```

Useful options

- -p Use the primary selection (default).

- -s Use the secondary selection.

- -b Use the clipboard selection.

- -i   Read the selection contents from standard input. This is the default behavior.

- -a   Append to the selection.

- -o   Write the selection contents to standard output.

- -c   Clear the selection contents.

- -x   Swap (exchange) the contents of the primary and secondary selection.

Math and Calculations

expr   Do simple math on the command line.

bc   Text-based calculator.

dc   Text-based RPN calculator.

Need a calculator? Linux provides some command-line programs to compute mathematical truths for you.

---

expr   stdin   **stdout**   - file   -- opt   **--help**   **--version**

expr *expression*

The expr command does simple math (and other expression evaluation) on the command line:

```
→ expr 7 + 3
10
→ expr '(' 7 + 3 ')' '*' 14        Shell characters are quoted
140
→ expr length ABCDEFG
7
→ expr 15 '>' 16
0                                  Meaning false
```

Each argument must be separated by whitespace. Notice that we had to quote or escape any characters that have special

---

meaning to the shell. Parentheses (escaped) may be used for grouping. Operators for expr include:

Operator	Numeric operation	String operation
+, -, *, /	Addition, subtraction, multiplication, and integer division, respectively	
%	Remainder (mod)	
<	Less than	Earlier in dictionary
<=	Less than or equal	Earlier in dictionary, or equal
>	Greater than	Later in dictionary
>=	Greater than or equal	Later in dictionary, or equal
=	Equality	Equality
!=	Inequality	Inequality
|	Boolean "or"	Boolean "or"
&	Boolean "and"	Boolean "and"
s : regexp		Does the regular expression regexp match string s?
substr s p n		Print n characters of string s, beginning at position p (p =1 is the first character)
index s chars		Return the index of the first position in string s containing a character from string chars. Return 0 if not found. Same behavior as the C function index( ).

For Boolean expressions, the number 0 and the empty string are considered false; any other value is true. For Boolean results, 0 is false and 1 is true.

bc [*options*] [*files*]

bc is a text-based calculator that reads arithmetic expressions, one per line, and prints the results. Unlike most other calculators, bc can handle numbers of unlimited size and any number of decimal places:

```
→ bc
1+2+3+4+5
15
scale=2
(1 + 2 * 3 / 4) - 5
-2.50
2^100
1267650600228229401496703205376
^D
```

Programmers may enjoy the ability to switch bases to perform calculations and conversions in binary, octal, hexadecimal, or even custom bases:

```
→ bc
obase=2              Display results in base 2
999
1111100111
obase=16             Or base 16
999
3E7
```

But bc doesn't stop there. It's also a programmable calculator in which you can define your own functions. Here's a function that implements the quadratic formula from algebra and prints the real roots of a given equation, stored in a file called *quadratic.txt*:[22]

---

22 This demonstration code will fail if the roots are imaginary.

```
→ cat quadratic.txt
scale=2
define quadform ( a, b, c ) {
 root1 = (-b + sqrt(b^2 - 4*a*c)) / (2*a)
 root2 = (-b - sqrt(b^2 - 4*a*c)) / (2*a)
 print root1, "  ", root2, "\n"
}

quadform(1, 7, 12)      solve x^2 + 7x + 12 = 0
```

Redirect the file to bc, and see the results:

```
→ bc < quadratic.txt
    -3.00   -4.00
```

In its most powerful form, bc is a programming language for arithmetic. You can assign values to variables, manipulate arrays, execute conditional expressions and loops, and even write scripts that prompt the user for values and run any sequence of math operations you like. For full details, see the manpage.

Useful arithmetic operations

`+, -, *, /`	Addition, subtraction, multiplication, and division, respectively. Results of division are truncated to the current scale (see below).
`%`	Remainder (mod).
`^`	Exponentiation, as in `10^5` for "ten to the fifth power."
`sqrt(N)`	Square root of N.
`ibase=N`	Treat all input numbers as base N.
`obase=N`	Output all numbers in base N.
`scale=N`	Set the number of significant digits after the decimal point to N.
`( ... )`	Parentheses for grouping (changing precedence).
`name=value`	Assign a value to the variable *name*.

dc stdin stdout - file -- opt --help --version

dc [*options*] [*files*]

The dc (desk calculator) command is a reverse-polish notation (RPN), stack-based calculator that reads expressions from standard input and writes results to standard output. If you know how to use a Hewlett-Packard RPN calculator, dc is pretty easy to use once you understand its syntax. But if you're accustomed to traditional calculators, dc may seem inscrutable. We'll cover only some basic commands.

For stack and calculator operations:

q   Quit dc.

f   Print the entire stack.

c   Delete (clear) the entire stack.

p   Print the topmost value on the stack.

P   Pop (remove) the topmost value from the stack.

n k   Set precision of future operations to be *n* decimal places (default is 0, meaning integer operations).

To pop the top two values from the stack, perform a requested operation, and push the result:

+, -, *, /   Addition, subtraction, multiplication, and division, respectively.

%   Remainder (mod).

^   Exponentiation (second-to-top value is the base, top value is the exponent).

To pop the top value from the stack, perform a requested operation, and push the result:

v   Square root.

Examples:

```
→ dc
4 5 + p          Print the sum of 4 and 5
9
2 3 ^ p          Raise 2 to the 3rd power and print the result
8
10 * p           Multiply the stack top by 10 and print the result
80
f                Print the stack
80
9
+p               Pop the top two values and print their sum
89
```

Dates and Times

cal   Print a calendar.

date   Print or set the date and time.

ntpdate   Set the system time using a remote timeserver.

Need a date? How about a good time? Try these programs to
display and set dates and times on your system.

---

cal   stdin   **stdout**   - file   -- opt   --help   --version

cal [*options*] [*month* [*year*]]

The cal command prints a calendar—by default, the current
month:

```
→ cal
November 2015
Su Mo Tu We Th Fr Sa
 1  2  3  4  5  6  7
 8  9 10 11 12 13 14
15 16 17 18 19 20 21
22 23 24 25 26 27 28
29 30
```

To print a different calendar, supply a month and four-digit year: cal 8 2016. If you omit the month (cal 2016), the entire year is printed.

Useful options

- -y   Print the current year's calendar.

- -3   Three-month view: print the previous and next month as well.

- -j   Number each day by its position in the year; in our example, February 1 would be displayed as 32, February 2 as 33, and so on.

---

date   stdin   **stdout**   - file   -- opt   **--help**   **--version**

date [*options*] [*format*]

The date command prints dates and times. The results will depend on your system's locale settings (for your country and language). In this section, we assume an English, US-based locale.

By default, date prints the system date and time in the local timezone:

```
→ date
Fri Mar 18 22:32:04 EDT 2016
```

You can format the output differently by supplying a format string beginning with a plus sign:

```
→ date '+%D'
03/18/16
→ date '+The time is %l:%M %p on a lovely %A in %B'
The time is 10:32 PM on a lovely Friday in March
```

Here is a sampling of the date command's many formats:

Format	Meaning	Example (US English)
Whole dates and times:		
%c	Full date and time, 12-hour clock	Sun 28 Sep 2003, 09:01:25 PM EDT
%D	Numeric date, 2-digit year	09/28/03
%x	Numeric date, 4-digit year	09/28/2003
%T	Time, 24-hour clock	21:01:25
%X	Time, 12-hour clock	09:01:25 PM
Words:		
%a	Day of week (abbreviated)	Sun
%A	Day of week (complete)	Sunday
%b	Month name (abbreviated)	Sep
%B	Month name (complete)	September
%Z	Time zone	EDT
%p	AM or PM	PM
Numbers:		
%w	Day of week (0–6, 0=Sunday)	0
%u	Day of week (1–7, 1=Monday)	7
%d	Day of month, leading zero	02
%e	Day of month, leading blank	2
%j	Day of year, leading zeros	005
%m	Month number, leading zero	09
%y	Year, 2 digits	03
%Y	Year, 4 digits	2003
%M	Minute, leading zero	09
%S	Seconds, leading zero	05
%l	Hour, 12-hour clock, leading blank	9

Format	Meaning	Example (US English)
%I	Hour, 12-hour clock, leading zero	09
%k	Hour, 24-hour clock, leading blank	9
%H	Hour, 24-hour clock, leading zero	09
%N	Nanoseconds	737418000
%s	Seconds since the beginning of Linux time: midnight January 1, 1970	1068583983
Other:		
%n	Newline character	
%t	Tab character	
%%	Percent sign	%

Through its options, date can also display other dates and times.

Useful options

-d *string*	Display the given date or time *string*, formatted as you wish.
-r *filename*	Display the last-modified timestamp of the given file, formatted as you wish.
-s *string*	Set the system date and/or time to be *string*; only the superuser can do this.

---

ntpdate　　　　stdin　**stdout**　- file　-- opt　--help　--version

ntpdate *timeserver*

The ntpdate command sets the current system time by contacting a timeserver machine on the network (you must be root to set the system time):

```
→ sudo /usr/sbin/ntpdate timeserver.someplace.edu
7 Sep 21:01:25 ntpdate[2399]: step time server
  178.99.1.8
offset 0.51 sec
```

To keep your system date in sync with a timeserver over long periods, use the daemon ntpd instead; see *http://www.ntp.org*. If you don't know a local timeserver, search the Web for "public ntp time server".

Graphics

display   Display a graphics file.

convert   Convert files from one graphical format into another.

mogrify   Modify a graphics file.

montage   Combine graphics files.

For viewing or editing graphics, Linux has handy tools with tons of options. We'll focus on command-line tools from a package called ImageMagick (*http://imagemagick.org*). Its commands all have similar usage, and a full explanation is at *http://imagemagick.org/script/command-line-processing.php*.

---

display   stdin   stdout   - file   -- opt   --help   --version

display [*options*] *files*

The display command lets you view images in numerous formats: JPEG, PNG, GIF, BMP, and more. It also includes a small suite of image editing tools that appear if you left-click the displayed image. Type q to exit the program.

→ **display photo.jpg**

The command is very powerful, with more than 100 options listed on its manpage.

Useful options

-resize *size*   Resize the image. The *size* values are extremely flexible, including setting the width (800), the height (x600), both (800x600), a percentage to grow or shrink (50%), an area in pixels (480000@), and more.

-flip   Reverse the image vertically.

-flop   Reverse the image horizontally.

-rotate *N*   Rotate the image by *N* degrees.

-backdrop   Display the image on a backdrop of solid color that covers the rest of your screen.

-fill   Set the solid color used by the -backdrop option.

-delay *N*   Show the image for *N* seconds and then exit. If you list multiple images, you get a slideshow with a delay of *N* seconds between images.

-identify   Print information about the image's format, size, and other statistics to standard output.

---

convert   stdin   stdout   -file   --opt   --help   --version

convert [*input_options*] *infile* [*output_options*] *outfile*

The convert command makes a copy of an image but converted to a different graphics format. For example, if you have a JPEG file, you can produce a PNG file of the same image:

→ **convert photo.jpg newphoto.png**

At the same time, you can perform modifications on the copy, such as resizing or reversing it:

→ **convert photo.jpg -resize 50% -flip newphoto.png**

convert accepts largely the same options as display.

---

mogrify

```
mogrify [options] file
```

The mogrify command transforms an image just like convert does, but the changes are made directly to the image file you provide, not in a copy. (So convert is a safer command when experimenting on a favorite photo.) It accepts largely the same options as convert:

```
→ mogrify -resize 25% photo.jpg
```

montage

```
montage infiles [options] outfile
```

montage produces a single image file from a collection of input files. For example, you can create a sheet of thumbnails in a single image, where each thumbnail is labeled with its original filename:

```
→ montage photo.jpg photo2.png photo3.gif \
  -geometry 120x176+10+10 -label '%f' outfile.jpg
```

montage provides great control over how those images appear. The preceding command, for example, produces thumbnails of size 120x176 pixels, offset by 10 pixels horizontally and vertically (creating space between the thumbnails), and labeled with their input filename.

Useful options

-geometry *widthxheight*[+-]*x*[+-]*y*	Set the height, width, and *(x, y)* offset of the images.
-frame *N*	Draw a frame of *N* pixels around each image.

`-label` *string*	Label each image with any *string*, which can contain special escape characters beginning with a percent sign: %f for the original filename, %h and %w for height and width, %m for file format, and about 40 others.

Audio and Video

`cdparanoia`	Rip audio from CDs to WAV files.
`lame`	Convert from WAV to MP3.
`id3info`	View ID3 tags in an MP3 file.
`id3tag`	Edit ID3 tags in an MP3 file.
`ogginfo`	View information about an OGG file.
`metaflac`	View and edit information about a FLAC file.
`sox`	Convert between audio file formats.
`mplayer`	Play a video or audio file.

There are numerous Linux programs with graphical interfaces for playing and editing audio and video, but we'll focus once again on command-line tools.

---

cdparanoia   stdin   stdout   - file   -- opt   --help   --version

`cdparanoia [options] span [outfile]`

The `cdparanoia` command reads (rips) audio data from a CD and stores it in WAV files (or other formats: see the manpage). Common uses are:

→ **cdparanoia** *N*
  Rip track *N* to a file.

→ **cdparanoia -B**

Rip all tracks on the CD into separate files.

→ **cdparanoia -B 2-4**

Rip tracks 2, 3, and 4 into separate files.

→ **cdparanoia 2-4**

Rip tracks 2, 3, and 4 into a single file.

If you experience difficulty with accessing your drive, try running cdparanoia -Qvs ("search for CD-ROM drives verbosely") and look for clues.

---

lame   stdin   stdout   **- file**   -- opt   **--help**   **--version**

lame [*options*] *file*.wav

The lame command converts a WAV audio file (say, *song.wav*) into an MP3 file:

→ **lame song.wav song.mp3**

It has over 100 options to control bit rate, convert other formats, add ID3 tags, and much more.

---

id3info   stdin   stdout   - file   -- opt   **--help**   **--version**

id3info [*options*] [*files*]

The id3info command displays information about an MP3 audio file, such as the song title, recording artist, album name, and year. This assumes the file has ID3 tags inside it. There are no options except displaying a help message and the program version:

→ **id3info guitar.mp3**
*** Tag information for guitar.mp3

```
=== TYER (Year): 2004
=== TCON (Content type): Sample File
=== TPE1 (Lead performer(s)/Soloist(s)): Gentle Giant
=== TIT2 (Title/songname): Guitar Solo
=== TALB (Album/Movie/Show title): Scraping the Barrel
*** mp3 info
MPEG1/layer III
Bitrate: 256KBps
Frequency: 44KHz
```

---

id3tag

stdin   stdout   - file   -- opt   --help   --version

id3tag [*options*] *files*

The id3tag command adds or modifies ID3 tags in an MP3 file. For example, to tag an MP3 file with a new title and artist, run:

→ **id3tag -A "My Album" -a "Loud Linux Squad" song.mp3**

Useful options

- -A *name*   Set the artist's name.

- -a *title*   Set the album title.

- -s *title*   Set the song title.

- -y *year*   Set the year.

- -t *number*   Set the track number.

- -g *number*   Set the genre number.

ogginfo

ogginfo [*options*] [*files*]

ogginfo is a simple command that displays information about an OGG Vorbis audio file:

```
→ ogginfo guitar.ogg
Processing file "guitar.ogg"...
...
Channels: 2
Rate: 44100
...
Nominal bitrate: 112.000000 kb/s
User comments section follows...
        Title=Guitar Solo
        Artist=Gentle Giant
        Album=Scraping the Barrel
        Year=2004
        Genre=Sample File
Vorbis stream 1:
        Total data length: 102390 bytes
        Playback length: 0m:09.952s
        Average bitrate: 82.301673 kb/s
```

Add the -h option for more detailed usage information.

metaflac

metaflac [*options*] [*files*]

The metaflac command displays or changes information about a FLAC audio file. To display information, run:

```
→ metaflac --list guitar.flac
...
  sample_rate: 44100 Hz
  channels: 2
```

```
    bits-per-sample: 16
    total samples: 438912
...
    comments: 5
        comment[0]: Title=Guitar Solo
        comment[1]: Artist=Gentle Giant
        comment[2]: Album=Scraping the Barrel
        comment[3]: Year=2004
        comment[4]: Genre=Sample File
```

The simplest way to change information, such as the title and artist, is to export the information to a text file, edit the file, and then reimport it:

```
→ metaflac --export-tags-to info.txt guitar.flac
→ cat info.txt
Title=Guitar Solo
Artist=Gentle Giant
Album=Scraping the Barrel
Year=2004
Genre=Sample File
→ nano info.txt        Make changes and save the file
→ metaflac --import-tags-from info.txt guitar.flac
```

Useful options

--show-tag *name*   Display the value for the given tag, such as title,
                      artist, album, year, etc. There are many other
                      "show" options for other information: see the
                      manpage.

--remove-tag *name*   Remove all occurrences of the given tag (title,
                      artist, etc.) from the FLAC file.

```
sox [options] infile outfile
```

sox is the simplest command for converting from one audio file format to another. MP3, OGG, FLAC, WAV, and dozens of other formats are supported. (Run man soxformat for a list.) Simply specify the new format using the correct file extension:

→ **sox guitar.mp3 guitar2.wav**   *MP3 to WAV*
→ **sox guitar.ogg guitar2.mp3**   *OGG to MP3*
→ **sox guitar.flac guitar2.ogg**   *FLAC to OGG*
...*and so forth*...

sox has *many* other uses, including combining audio files and adding special effects; it's often called the "Swiss Army knife" of audio commands. See the manpage for details.

Useful options

-S	Show a progress meter; useful for long conversions.
--no-clobber	Don't overwrite the output file if it already exists.
-t *type*	Specify the type of the input file, if sox cannot figure it out. See man soxformat for the list of types.

---

mplayer   stdin   stdout -file -- opt --help --version

```
mplayer [options] video_files...
```

The mplayer command plays video files in many formats (MPEG, AVI, MOV, and more):

→ **mplayer myfile.avi**

While the video is playing, press the space bar to pause and resume, the cursor keys to jump forward and backward in time, and Q to quit. mplayer also plays audio files. The program has dozens of options on its manpage, and you can learn more at *http://www.mplayerhq.hu*.

Other popular video players for Linux include vlc (*http://www.videolan.org/vlc/*), kaffeine (*http://kaffeine.kde.org/*), and xine (*http://www.xine-project.org/*).

Installing Software

You will probably want to add further software to your Linux system from time to time. The method of installation varies, however, because Linux has multiple standards for "packaged" software. Your distro might perform installations on the command line, with one or more GUI tools, or both. The most common package types are:

*.deb files
> Debian packages, used by Debian, Ubuntu, and other distros. We'll cover the package management commands aptitude, apt-get, and dpkg for installing software in this format.

*.rpm files
> RPM Package Manager files are used by Red Hat, Fedora, CentOS, and other distros. These are installed by the package managers dnf, yum, and rpm.

*.tar.gz files and *.tar.bz2 files
> Compressed tar files. This kind of file isn't an installable "package" but a collection of files created by tar and compressed with gzip (*.gz*) or bzip2 (*.bz2*). Whereas Debian and RPM packages can be installed with a single command, compressed tar files usually require multiple manual steps.

You must learn which package type is used by your Linux system. In general, you cannot (or should not) mix package types like Debian and RPM. Fortunately, modern Linux systems are usually set up with a package manager when initially installed, so all you need to do is use it.

If you aren't sure which Linux distro you're running, one of the following commands should give you a clue:

```
→ cat /etc/issue
Ubuntu 15.10 \n \l
→ more /etc/*-release
NAME="Ubuntu"
VERSION="15.10 (Wily Werewolf)"
...
```

Most new software must be installed by the superuser, so you'll need to run the sudo command (or equivalent) for any installation. For example:

```
→ sudo rpm -ivh mypackage.rpm
Password: ********
```

Your Linux distribution almost certainly comes with graphical programs for manipulating packages, but you may find the command-line programs to be simpler or faster depending on your needs.

---

dnf   stdin   **stdout**   - file   -- opt   **--help**   **--version**

dnf [*options*] [*packages*]

dnf is the newest package manager for RPM packages (*.rpm* files).

The following table lists common operations with `dnf`:

Action	dnf command
Search for a package that meets your needs (supports wildcards * and ?)	`dnf search command_name`
Check if a package is installed	`dnf list installed package_name`
Download a package but don't install it	`dnf download package_name`
Download and install a package	`sudo dnf install package_name`
Install a package file	`sudo dnf install file.rpm`
Learn about a package	`dnf info package_name`
List the contents of a package	`rpm -ql package_name`
Discover which package an installed file belongs to	`dnf provides /path/to/file`
Update an installed package	`sudo dnf upgrade package_name`
Remove an installed package	`sudo dnf remove package_name`
List all packages installed on the system	`dnf list installed	less`
Check for updates for all packages on the system	`dnf check-update`
Update all packages on the system	`sudo dnf upgrade`

yum   stdin   **stdout**   - file   -- opt   **--help**   **--version**

yum [*options*] [*packages*]

yum is a popular package manager for RPM packages (*.rpm* files) found on Red Hat Enterprise Linux, Fedora, CentOS, and other distros. It is primarily a command-line tool, though you may encounter graphical frontends for yum, such as PackageKit on Fedora Linux.

The following table lists common operations with yum. For operations on local files, which yum does not provide, we use the rpm command directly:

Action	yum command
Search for a package that meets your needs (supports wildcards * and ?)	yum search *command_name*
Check if a package is installed	yum list installed *package_name*

Download a package but don't install it. Requires the downloadonly plugin; to install it, run:
  sudo yum install \\
  yum-downloadonly
	sudo yum --downloadonly install *package_name*

Download and install a package	sudo yum install *package_name*
Install a package file	rpm -ivh *package*.rpm
Learn about a package	yum info *package_name*
List the contents of a package	rpm -ql *package_name*
Discover which package an installed file belongs to	yum provides */path/to/ file*

Action	yum command
Update an installed package	`sudo yum update package_name`
Remove an installed package	`sudo yum remove package_name`
List all packages installed on the system	`yum list installed	less`
Check for updates for all packages on the system	`yum check-update`
Update all packages on the system	`sudo yum update`

rpm   stdin   **stdout**   - file   -- opt   **--help**   **--version**

`rpm [options] [files]`

If you prefer to download and install RPM packages by hand, use rpm, the same package-management program that yum runs behind the scenes. Unlike yum, rpm works locally on your computer: it does not search software archives on the Internet for new packages.

rpm not only installs the software, but also confirms that your system has all prerequisites. For example, if package *superstuff* requires package *otherstuff* that you haven't installed, rpm will not install *superstuff*. If your system passes the test, however, rpm installs the requested package.

RPM filenames typically take the following form *<name>-<version>.<architecture>.rpm*. For example, the filename *emacs-23.1-17.i386.rpm* indicates the emacs package, version 23.1-17, for i386 (Intel 80386 and higher) machines. Be aware that rpm sometimes requires a filename argument (like *emacs-23.1-17.i386.rpm*) and other times just the package name (like *emacs*).

Action	rpm command
Check if a package is installed	`rpm -q package_name`
Install a package file	`sudo rpm -ivh package_file.rpm`
Learn about a package	`rpm -qi package_name`
List the contents of a package	`rpm -ql package_name`
Discover which package an installed file belongs to	`rpm -qf /path/to/file`
Update an installed package	`sudo rpm -Uvh package_file.rpm`
Remove an installed package	`sudo rpm -e package_name`
List all packages installed on the system	`rpm -qa	less`

APT   stdin stdout - file -- opt --help --version

`apt-get [options] packages`

`apt-file [options] string`

`apt-cache [options] packages`

`dpkg [options] packages`

The APT (Advanced Packaging Tool) suite of commands can install, remove, and manipulate Debian (*.deb*) packages.

Before upgrading packages on your system, run `sudo apt-get update` to retrieve the latest information on which packages are available.

Action	APT command
Search for a package that meets your needs	`apt-file search package_name`
Check if a package is installed	`dpkg -s package_name`
Download a package but don't install it	`apt-get -d package_name`
Download and install a package	`sudo apt-get install package_name`
Install a package file	`dpkg -i package_file.deb`
Learn about a package	`apt-cache show package_name`
List the contents of a package	`dpkg -L package_name`
Discover which package an installed file belongs to	`dpkg -S /path/to/file`
Update an installed package	`sudo apt-get upgrade package_name`
Remove an installed package	`sudo apt-get remove package_name`
List all packages installed on the system	`dpkg -l`
Check for updates for all packages on the system	`sudo apt-get -u upgrade`
Update all packages on the system (to include kernel packages, replace upgrade by dist-upgrade)	`sudo apt-get upgrade`

```
aptitude [options] [packages]
```

aptitude is another package manager for the command line that manipulates Debian (*.deb*) packages. You'll also need to know dpkg for some operations, such as working with local *.deb* files, as aptitude does not have that capability.

Action	aptitude command
Search for a package that meets your needs	`aptitude search package_name`
Check if a package is installed (examine the output for "State: not installed" or "State: installed")	`aptitude show package_name`
Download a package but don't install it	`aptitude download package_name`
Download and install a package	`sudo aptitude install package_name`
Install a package file	`dpkg -i package_file.deb`
Learn about a package	`aptitude show package_name`
List the contents of a package	`dpkg -L package_name`
Discover which package an installed file belongs to	`dpkg -S /path/to/file`
Update an installed package	`sudo aptitude safe-upgrade package_name`
Remove an installed package	`sudo aptitude remove package_name`
List all packages installed on the system	`aptitude search '~i' | less`

Action	aptitude command
Check for updates for all packages on the system	`aptitude --simulate full-upgrade`
Update all packages on the system	`sudo aptitude full-upgrade`

tar.gz and tar.bz2 Files

Packaged software files with names ending *.tar.gz* and *.tar.bz2* typically contain source code that you'll need to compile (build) before installation. Typical build instructions are:

1. List the package contents, one file per line. Assure yourself that each file, when extracted, won't overwrite something precious on your system, either accidentally or maliciously:[23]

   ```
   → tar tvf package.tar.gz | less        gzip
   → tar tvf package.tar.bz2 | less       bzip2
   ```

2. If satisfied, extract the files into a new directory. Run these commands as yourself, not as root, for safety reasons:

   ```
   → mkdir newdir
   → cd installation_directory
   → tar xvf <path>/package.tar.gz        gzip
   → tar xvf <path>/package.tar.bz2       bzip2
   ```

3. Look for an extracted file named *INSTALL* or *README*. Read it to learn how to build the software, for example:

   ```
   → cd newdir
   → less INSTALL
   ```

---

23 A maliciously designed tar file could include an absolute file path like */etc/passwd* designed to overwrite your system password file.

4. Usually the *INSTALL* or *README* file will tell you to run a script called `configure` in the current directory, then run `make`, then run `make install`. Examine the options you may pass to the `configure` script:

    ```
    → ./configure --help
    ```

    Then install the software:

    ```
    → ./configure options
    → make
    → sudo make install
    ```

Programming with Shell Scripts

Earlier when we covered the shell (bash), we said it had a programming language built in. In fact, you can write programs, or *shell scripts*, to accomplish tasks that a single command cannot. The command `reset-lpg`, supplied in the book's examples directory, is a shell script that you can read:

```
→ less ~/linuxpocketguide/reset-lpg
```

Like any good programming language, the shell has variables, conditionals (if-then-else), loops, input and output, and more. Entire books have been written on shell scripting, so we'll be covering the bare minimum to get you started. For full documentation, run `info bash`, search the Web, or pick up a more in-depth O'Reilly book like *Learning the bash Shell* or *Bash Pocket Reference*.

Creating and Running Shell Scripts

To create a shell script, simply put bash commands into a file as you would type them. To run the script, you have three choices:

Prepend #!/bin/bash and make the file executable
  This is the most common way to run scripts. Add the line:

  ```
  #!/bin/bash
  ```

to the very top of the script file. It must be the first line of the file, left-justified. Then make the file executable:

```
→ chmod +x myscript
```

Optionally, move it into a directory in your search path. Then run it like any other command:

```
→ myscript
```

If the script is in your current directory, but the current directory "." is not in your search path, you'll need to prepend "./" so the shell finds the script:

```
→ ./myscript
```

The current directory is generally not in your search path for security reasons. (You wouldn't want a local script named (say) "ls" to override the real ls command.)

Pass to bash

bash will interpret its argument as the name of a script and run it.

```
→ bash myscript
```

Run in current shell with "." or source

The preceding methods run your script as an independent entity that has no effect on your current shell.[24] If you want your script to make changes to your current shell (setting variables, changing directory, etc.), it can be run in the current shell with the source or "." command:

```
→ . myscript
→ source myscript
```

---

24 That's because the script runs in a separate shell (a *subshell* or *child shell*) that cannot alter the original shell.

Whitespace and Linebreaks

Bash shell scripts are very sensitive to whitespace and linebreaks. Because the "keywords" of this programming language are actually commands evaluated by the shell, you need to separate arguments with whitespace. Likewise, a linebreak in the middle of a command will mislead the shell into thinking the command is incomplete. Follow the conventions we present here and you should be fine.

If you must break a long command into multiple lines, end each line (except the last) with a single \ character, which means "continued on next line":

```
→ grep abcdefghijklmnopqrstuvwxyz file1 file2 \
  file3 file4
```

Variables

We described shell variables earlier:

```
→ MYVAR=6
→ echo $MYVAR
6
```

All values held in variables are strings, but if they are numeric, the shell will treat them as numbers when appropriate:

```
→ NUMBER="10"
→ expr $NUMBER + 5
15
```

When you refer to a variable's value in a shell script, it's a good idea to surround it with double quotes to prevent certain runtime errors. An undefined variable, or a variable with spaces in its value, will evaluate to something unexpected if not surrounded by quotes, causing your script to malfunction:

```
→ FILENAME="My Document"             Space in the name
→ ls $FILENAME                       Try to list it
ls: My: No such file or directory    ls saw 2 arguments
ls: Document: No such file or directory
```

```
→ ls -l "$FILENAME"                 List it properly
My Document                         ls saw only 1 argument
```

If a variable name is evaluated adjacent to another string, surround it with curly braces to prevent unexpected behavior:

```
→ HAT="fedora"
→ echo "The plural of $HAT is $HATs"
The plural of fedora is             No variable "HATs"
→ echo "The plural of $HAT is ${HAT}s"
The plural of fedora is fedoras     What we wanted
```

Input and Output

Script output is provided by the echo and printf commands, which we described in "Screen Output" on page 203:

```
→ echo "Hello world"
Hello world
→ printf "I am %d years old\n" `expr 20 + 20`
I am 40 years old
```

Input is provided by the read command, which reads one line from standard input and stores it in a variable:

```
→ read name
Sandy Smith <ENTER>
→ echo "I read the name $name"
I read the name Sandy Smith
```

Booleans and Return Codes

Before we can describe conditionals and loops, we need to explain the concept of a Boolean (true/false) test. To the shell, the value 0 means true or success, and anything else means false or failure. (Think of zero as "no error" and other values as error codes.)

Additionally, every Linux command returns an integer value, called a *return code* or *exit status*, to the shell when the command exits.

You can see this value in the special variable $?:

```
→ cat myfile
My name is Sandy Smith and
I really like Ubuntu Linux
→ grep Smith myfile
My name is Sandy Smith and        A match was found...
→ echo $?
0                                 ...so return code is "success"
→ grep aardvark myfile
→ echo $?                         No match was found...
1                                 ...so return code is "failure"
```

The return codes of a command are usually documented on its manpage.

test and "["

The test command (built into the shell) will evaluate simple Boolean expressions involving numbers and strings, setting its exit status to 0 (true) or 1 (false):

```
→ test 10 -lt 5        Is 10 less than 5?
→ echo $?
1                      No, it isn't
→ test -n "hello"      Does "hello" have nonzero length?
→ echo $?
0                      Yes, it does
```

Here are common test arguments for checking properties of integers, strings, and files:

File tests

-d *name*	File *name* is a directory
-f *name*	File *name* is a regular file
-L *name*	File *name* is a symbolic link
-r *name*	File *name* exists and is readable
-w *name*	File *name* exists and is writable
-x *name*	File *name* exists and is executable

`-s` *name*	File *name* exists and its size is nonzero
`f1` `-nt` `f2`	File *f1* is newer than file *f2*
`f1` `-ot` `f2`	File *f1* is older than file *f2*

String tests

`s1` `=` `s2`	String *s1* equals string *s2*
`s1` `!=` `s2`	String *s1* does not equal string *s2*
`-z` *s1*	String *s1* has zero length
`-n` *s1*	String *s1* has nonzero length

Numeric tests

`a` `-eq` `b`	Integers *a* and *b* are equal
`a` `-ne` `b`	Integers *a* and *b* are not equal
`a` `-gt` `b`	Integer *a* is greater than integer *b*
`a` `-ge` `b`	Integer *a* is greater than or equal to integer *b*
`a` `-lt` `b`	Integer *a* is less than integer *b*
`a` `-le` `b`	Integer *a* is less than or equal to integer *b*

Combining and negating tests

`t1` `-a` `t2`	And: Both tests t1 and t2 are true
`t1` `-o` `t2`	Or: Either test t1 or t2 is true
`!` *your_test*	Negate the test (i.e., your_test is false)
`\(` *your_test* `\)`	Parentheses are used for grouping, as in algebra

`test` has an unusual alias, "`[`" (left square bracket), as a shorthand for use with conditionals and loops. If you use this shorthand, you must supply a final argument of "`]`" (right square bracket) to signify the end of the test. The following tests are identical to the previous two:

```
→ [ 10 -lt 5 ]
→ echo $?
1
→ [ -n "hello" ]
```

```
→ echo $?
0
```

Remember that "[" is a command like any other, so it is followed by *individual arguments separated by whitespace.* So if you mistakenly forget some whitespace:

```
→ [ 5 -lt 4]          No space between 4 and ]
bash: [: missing ']'
```

then test thinks the final argument is the string "4]" and complains that the final bracket is missing.

A more powerful—but less portable—syntax for Boolean tests is the double bracket, [[, which adds regular expression matching and eliminates some of the quirks of test. See *http://mywiki.wooledge.org/BashFAQ/031* for details.

Conditionals

The if statement chooses between alternatives, each of which may have a complex test. The simplest form is the if-then statement:

```
if command          If exit status of command is 0
then
  body
fi
```

Here's an example script with an if statement:

```
→ cat script-if
#!/bin/bash
if [ `whoami` = "root" ]
then
  echo "You are the superuser"
fi
```

Next is the if-then-else statement:

```
if command
then
  body1
```

```
else
  body2
fi
```

For example:

```
→ cat script-else
#!/bin/bash
if [ `whoami` = "root" ]
then
  echo "You are the superuser"
else
  echo "You are a mere mortal"
fi
→ ./script-else
You are a mere mortal
→ sudo ./script-else
Password: ********
You are the superuser
```

Finally, we have the form if-then-elif-else, which may have as many tests as you like:

```
if command1
then
  body1
elif command2
then
  body2
elif ...
  ...
else
  bodyN
fi
```

For example:

```
→ cat script-elif
#!/bin/bash
bribe=20000
if [ `whoami` = "root" ]
then
  echo "You are the superuser"
```

```
elif [ "$USER" = "root" ]
then
  echo "You might be the superuser"
elif [ "$bribe" -gt 10000 ]
then
  echo "You can pay to be the superuser"
else
  echo "You are still a mere mortal"
fi
→ ./script-elif
You can pay to be the superuser
```

The case statement evaluates a single value and branches to an appropriate piece of code:

```
→ cat script-case
#!/bin/bash
echo -n "What would you like to do (eat, sleep)? "
read answer
case "$answer" in
  eat)
    echo "OK, have a hamburger."
    ;;
  sleep)
    echo "Good night then."
    ;;
  *)
    echo "I'm not sure what you want to do."
    echo "I guess I'll see you tomorrow."
    ;;
esac
→ ./script-case
What would you like to do (eat, sleep)? sleep
Good night then.
```

The general form is:

```
case string in
  expr1)
    body1
    ;;
  expr2)
```

```
    body2
    ;;
  ...
  exprN)
    bodyN
    ;;
  *)
    bodyelse
    ;;
esac
```

where *string* is any value, usually a variable value like $myvar, and *expr1* through *exprN* are patterns (run the command info bash for details), with the final * like a final "else." Each set of commands must be terminated by ;; (as shown):

```
→ cat script-case2
#!/bin/bash
echo -n "Enter a letter: "
read letter
case $letter in
  X)
    echo "$letter is an X"
    ;;
  [aeiou])
    echo "$letter is a vowel"
    ;;
  [0-9])
    echo "$letter is a digit, silly"
    ;;
  *)
    echo "The letter '$letter' is not supported"
    ;;
esac
→ ./script-case2
Enter a letter: e
e is a vowel
```

Loops

The while loop repeats a set of commands as long as a condition is true.

```
while command          While the exit status of command is 0
do
  body
done
```

For example:

```
→ cat script-while
#!/bin/bash
i=0
while [ $i -lt 3 ]
do
  echo "$i"
  i=`expr $i + 1`
done
→ ./script-while
0
1
2
```

The until loop repeats until a condition becomes true:

```
until command     While the exit status of command is nonzero
do
  body
done
```

For example:

```
→ cat script-until
#!/bin/bash
i=0
until [ $i -ge 3 ]
do
  echo "$i"
  i=`expr $i + 1`
done
→ ./script-until
```

```
0
1
2
```

Be careful to avoid infinite loops, using `while` with a condition that always evaluates to 0 (true), or `until` with a condition that always evaluates to a nonzero value (false):

```
i=1
while [ $i -lt 10 ]        Variable i never changes. Infinite!
do
  echo "forever"
done
```

Another type of loop, the `for` loop, iterates over values from a list:

```
for variable in list
do
  body
done
```

For example:

```
→ cat script-for
#!/bin/bash
for name in Tom Jane Harry
do
  echo "$name is my friend"
done
→ ./script-for
Tom is my friend
Jane is my friend
Harry is my friend
```

The `for` loop is particularly handy for processing lists of files; for example, filenames with a certain extension in the current directory:

```
→ cat script-for2
#!/bin/bash
for file in *.docx
do
```

```
    echo "$file is a stinky Microsoft Word file"
done
→ ./script-for2
letter.docx is a stinky Microsoft Word file
```

You can also use the seq command (see seq on page 208) to produce a list of consecutive integers, and then loop over those numbers:

```
→ cat script-seq
#!/bin/bash
for i in $(seq 1 20)    Generates the numbers 1 2 3 4 ... 20
do
   echo "iteration $i"
done
→ ./script-seq
iteration 1
iteration 2
iteration 3
...
iteration 20
```

Command-Line Arguments

Shell scripts can accept command-line arguments and options just like other Linux commands. (In fact, some common Linux commands *are* scripts.) Within your shell script, you can refer to these arguments as $1, $2, $3, and so on:

```
→ cat script-args
#!/bin/bash
echo "My name is $1 and I come from $2"

→ ./script-args Johnson Wisconsin
My name is Johnson and I come from Wisconsin
→ ./script-args Bob
My name is Bob and I come from
```

Your script can test the number of arguments it received with $#:

```
→ cat script-args2
#!/bin/bash
if [ $# -lt 2 ]
then
  echo "$0 error: you must supply two arguments"
else
  echo "My name is $1 and I come from $2"
fi
```

The special value $0 contains the name of the script, and is handy for usage and error messages:

```
→ ./script-args2 Barbara
./script-args2 error: you must supply two arguments
```

To iterate over all command-line arguments, use a for loop with the special variable $@, which holds all arguments:

```
→ cat script-args3
#!/bin/bash
for arg in $@
do
  echo "I found the argument $arg"
done
→ ./script-args3 One Two Three
I found the argument One
I found the argument Two
I found the argument Three
```

Exiting with a Return Code

The exit command terminates your script and passes a given return code to the shell. By tradition, scripts should return 0 for success and 1 (or other nonzero value) on failure. If your script doesn't call exit, the return code is automatically 0:

```
→ cat script-exit
#!/bin/bash
if [ $# -lt 2 ]
then
  echo "$0 error: you must supply two arguments"
  exit 1
```

```
else
  echo "My name is $1 and I come from $2"
fi
exit 0
```

```
→ ./script-exit Bob
./script-exit error: you must supply two arguments
→ echo $?
1
```

Piping to bash

Bash is not just a shell; it's also a command, bash, that reads from standard input. This means you can construct commands as strings and send them to bash for execution:

```
→ echo wc -l myfile
wc -l myfile
→ echo wc -l myfile | bash
18 myfile
```

Bash Warning

Piping commands into bash is powerful but can also be dangerous. First make sure you know *exactly* which commands will be executed. You don't want to pipe an unexpected rm command to bash and delete a valuable file (or 1,000 valuable files).

If someone asks you to retrieve a web page (say, with the curl command) and pipe it blindly into bash, don't do it! Instead, capture the web page as a file (with curl or wget), examine it closely, and make an informed decision whether to execute it with bash.

This technique is incredibly useful. Suppose you want to download the files *photo1.jpg*, *photo2.jpg*, through *photo100.jpg* from a website. Instead of typing 100 wget commands by hand, construct the commands with a loop, using seq to construct the list of integers from 1 to 100:

```
→ for i in `seq 1 100`
do
  echo wget http://example.com/photo$i.jpg
done
wget http://example.com/photo1.jpg
wget http://example.com/photo2.jpg
...
wget http://example.com/photo100.jpg
```

Yes, you've constructed the text of 100 commands. Now pipe the output to bash, which will run all 100 commands as if you'd typed them by hand:

```
→ for i in `seq 1 100`
do
  echo wget http://example.com/photo$i.jpg
done | bash
```

Here's a more complex but practical application. Suppose you have a set of files you want to rename. Put the old names into a file *oldnames*, and the new names into a file *newnames*:

```
→ cat oldnames
oldname1
oldname2
oldname3
→ cat newnames
newname1
newname2
newname3
```

Now use the commands paste and sed ("File Text Manipulation" on page 93) to place the old and new names side by side and prepend the word "mv" to each line, and the output is a sequence of "mv" commands:

```
→ cat oldnames | paste -d' ' oldnames newnames \
  | sed 's/^/mv /'
mv oldfile1 newfile1
mv oldfile2 newfile2
mv oldfile3 newfile3
```

Finally, pipe the output to bash, and the renaming takes place!

```
→ cat oldnames | paste -d' ' oldnames newnames \
  | sed 's/^/mv /' \
  | bash
```

Beyond Shell Scripting

Shell scripts are fine for many purposes, but Linux comes with much more powerful scripting languages, as well as compiled programming languages. Here are a few:

Language	Program	To get started...
C, C++	gcc, g++	man gcc *https://gcc.gnu.org/*
.NET	mono	man mono *http://www.mono-project.com/*
Java	javac	*http://java.com/*
Perl	perl	man perl *http://www.perl.com/*
PHP	php	man php *http://php.net/*
Python	python	man python *https://www.python.org/*
Ruby	ruby	*http://www.ruby-lang.org/*

Final Words

Although we've covered many commands and capabilities of Linux, we've just scratched the surface. Most distributions come with *thousands* of other programs. We encourage you to continue reading, exploring, and learning the capabilities of your Linux systems. Good luck!

Acknowledgments

I am very grateful to the many readers who purchased the first two editions of this book, making the third edition possible. My heartfelt thanks also go to my editor, Nan Barber, the O'Reilly production staff, the technical review team (Justin Karimi, Bill Ricker, Dan Ritter), Jay Moran at Cimpress, and as always, my beautiful family, Lisa and Sophia.

Index

About the Author

Daniel J. Barrett has been immersed in Internet technology since 1985. Currently a director of technology at an ecommerce company, Dan has also been a heavy metal singer, software engineer, system administrator, university lecturer, web designer, and humorist. He is the author of O'Reilly's *Linux Pocket Guide*, and he is the coauthor of *Linux Security Cookbook*, and *SSH, The Secure Shell: The Definitive Guide*.